Computer Science Principles

The Foundational Concepts of Computer Science
For AP® Computer Science

Kevin Hare

with a foreword by Pindar Van Arman

Yellow Dart Publishing

Second Edition

All inquiries should be addressed to:
Yellow Dart Publishing
PO Box 660502
Atlanta, GA 30366
www.apcompsciprinciples.com

Microsoft product screenshots used with permission from Microsoft

Adobe product screenshots reprinted with permission from Adobe Systems Incorporated.

Adobe®, Adobe® Dreamweaver®, and Adobe® Photoshop are either registered trademarks or trademarks of Adobe Systems Incorporated in the United States and/or other countries.

Google and the Google logo are registered trademarks of Google Inc., used with permission

AP® and Advanced Placement® are trademarks registered by the College Board, which was not involved in the production of, and does not endorse, this text.

ISBN: 978-0-692-10671-6

To Parker and Quinn,

01001001 00100000 01101100 01101111

01110110 01100101 00100000 01111001

01101111 01110101

-K.H.

Computer Science Principles

Foreword

I envy readers of this computer science textbook. It's not like the textbook I started out with. That book was filled with exercises that resembled mathematics problems. Algorithms were described along with demonstrations of the most efficient way to use them. We were then challenged to solve these problems in the most efficient way possible. It's not that these exercises weren't fun, but they were very rigid and usually had a single correct answer. This put creative types like me at a disadvantage. I wanted to experiment with software and try different approaches, even if they were not the best approaches. The textbook I remember was not designed for that. It emphasized efficiency over creativity.

But this textbook is different. Computer science is a creative field, and this textbook's approach celebrates this creativity. This textbook will put you well on your way to understanding how to use modern software applications, what makes them work, and how you can improve on them to write your own applications.

As an artist, I think this creative approach is the most interesting way to tackle any problem.

My art is a little unusual. I design creative algorithms then have several custom robots use these algorithms to create paintings, one brushstroke at a time. These AI generated paintings are a record of both how far I have come in the discipline of computational creativity, and how far artificial intelligence in general has developed.

My most recent painting robot project is called CloudPainter, and it can paint some wonderful paintings. I named it CloudPainter not because every new computer-related thing needs to have the word "cloud" in it, but because I want my latest robots to be able to look into the clouds and be inspired by them to create their artwork. We humans might notice that a cloud resembles a dragon and use that as inspiration to let our imaginations run wild. I wanted my robots to be able to do the exact same thing. I wanted them to imagine the images they painted.

We have had some success toward that goal. While my earliest robots were relatively simple machines that dipped a brush in paint and dragged the brush around a canvas, my most recent robots use dozens of artificial intelligence algorithms, a handful of deep-learning neural networks, and continuous feedback loops to paint with increasing creative autonomy.

Exactly how far has their creativity come?

Famed New York art critic Jerry Saltz recently reviewed one of my robotic paintings. Speaking of the Portrait of Elle Reeve, he began it "doesn't look like this was made by a computer." He then paused and continued, "That doesn't make it any good." It sounds like a bad review, but I loved it. A couple years ago, no one even considered our paintings to be art. Now people at least think they're bad art. That is progress!

To make a portrait that didn't look like a computer made it, my robots used all their creative abilities to re-imagine Elle Reeve's face in an abstract impressionistic style then painted it based on strokes modeled from a famous Picasso.

Jerry Saltz' admission that this painting could have been done by a human hand was a major milestone in my artistic career. As I mentioned, few have acknowledged my art as art at all. Some looked at my painting robots and called them over-engineered printers. Other naysayers complained that our paintings were little more than images run through the equivalent of a photoshop filter.

Beyond the robots and their paintings, people often took offense at the very idea of what I was trying to do, which was to create artistic robots. For many it was a grotesque attempt to mimic the very essence of what makes us human. My attempts threatened and worried people. I remember one exhibition where an artist pulled me over and said "I don't know whether to be impressed or disgusted with your work."

Over the years, however, there also have been many who understood exactly what I was trying to accomplish. The author of this book, Kevin Hare, was one of them. We first met while teaching in

Washington, DC. Kevin was a computer science teacher. I taught art. My friendship with Kevin was unexpected. Our classrooms were on opposite sides of campus, and one would think that there would be little overlap in our curriculum. As we got to know each other, however, it quickly became apparent that we were on similar wavelengths. We both realized the creative power of software. We had many conversations where we discussed the similarities between our creative processes. Both of us realized just how similar writing code was to making art.

As I read this book, I was reminded of many things he shared with me about the creative aspects of computer design. You will find it in his style as well as the exercises he provides. This book does not just ask you to complete a task for the sake of completing it. It challenges you to have fun with the code to do the things that you are interested in.

His concern for keeping your interest can even be seen in the order in which he covers the material. The book begins by introducing the basics, as would be expected, but then it does something unusual. The second chapter goes right into the creative side of software by exploring photo editing. As an artist, this made perfect sense to me. It even mirrored my own journey into computer science. The first programs I used were photo editing tools like Photoshop. As I needed these tools to do more than they were capable of, I found myself writing my own. This got me started in computer science and eventually led to my AI robots.

The truly fun part of computer science is learning how to use code to be better at the things you love. Kevin Hare understands this perfectly and goes out of his way to teach you things that have interesting practical applications.

At its core, software is a tool that helps us do things much more efficiently. Simple programs like word processors let us write more words per minute. Spreadsheets let us do complex accounting and analysis. More complex programs like Photoshop and Garage Band help us make art and compose music. Those of us who take the time to understand and master these tools have a great advantage over those who do not.

Do you like playing an instrument? Chapter six will help you make a website for your band. Like making art, like I do? Creative applications are discussed in multiple chapters, beginning with chapter two. Want to make billions of dollars creating the hot new crypto-currency? Look no further than chapter seven's discussion of cryptography.

Regardless of your interest, this book will get you started on the path to writing software that helps you excel. Making yourself better at whatever you want to be better at has never been easier.

Pindar Van Arman
Creator, *CloudPainter*
www.cloudpainter.com

About AP® Computer Science Principles

Course Description

AP Computer Science Principles offers a multidisciplinary approach to teaching the underlying principles of computation. The course will introduce students to the creative aspects of programming, abstractions, algorithms, large data sets, the Internet, cybersecurity concerns, and computing impacts. AP Computer Science Principles also gives students the opportunity to use current technologies to create computational artifacts for both self-expression and problem solving. Together, these aspects of the course make up a rigorous and rich curriculum that aims to broaden participation in computer science.

Course Goals and Learning Outcomes

The following are the major areas of study, or big ideas, that are foundational to studying computer science:

- **Creativity:** Computing is a creative activity. Creativity and computing are prominent forces in innovation; the innovations enabled by computing have had and will continue to have far-reaching impact.

- **Abstraction:** Abstraction reduces information and detail to facilitate focus on relevant concepts. It is a process, a strategy, and the result of reducing detail to focus on concepts relevant to understanding and solving problems.

- **Data and Information:** Data and information facilitate the creation of knowledge. Computing enables and empowers new methods of information processing, driving monumental change across many disciplines — from art to business to science.

- **Algorithms:** Algorithms are used to develop and express solutions to computational problems. Algorithms realized in software have affected the world in profound and lasting ways.

- **Programming:** Programming enables problem solving, human expression, and creation of knowledge. Programming and the creation of software has changed our lives. It results in the creation of software, and facilitates the creation of computational artifacts, such as music, images, and visualizations.

- **The Internet:** The Internet pervades modern computing. The Internet and the systems built on it have had a profound impact on society. Computer networks support communication and collaboration.

- **Global Impact:** Computing has global impact. Our methods for communicating, collaborating, problem solving, and doing business have changed and are changing due to innovations enabled by computing.

The course also incorporates computational thinking practices that set clear expectations of what students will do in the course:

- **Connecting Computing** – Students learn to draw connections between different computing concepts.

- **Creating computational artifacts** – Students engage in the creative aspects of computing by designing and developing interesting computational artifacts as well as by applying computing techniques to creatively solve problems.

- **Abstracting** – Students use abstraction to develop models and simulations of natural and artificial phenomena, use them to make predictions about the world, and analyze their efficacy and validity.

- **Analyzing problems and artifacts** – Students design and produce solutions, models, and artifacts, and they evaluate and analyze their own computational work as well as the computational work others have produced.

- **Communicating** – Students describe computation and the impact of technology and computation, explain and justify the design and appropriateness of their computational choices, and analyze and describe both computational artifacts and the results or behaviors of those artifacts.

- **Collaborating** – Students collaborate on a number of activities, including investigation of questions using data sets and in the production of computational artifacts.

Source:

AP Computer Science Principles Course Description
Copyright © 2018 The College Board.
Reproduced with permission.
http://apcentral.collegeboard.com

Readings, Materials, and Resources

- *Blown to Bits: Your Life, Liberty, and Happiness After the Digital Explosion*
  Harold Abelson, Ken Ledeen, Harry Lewis – Addison-Wesley – 2008

- *Nine Algorithms That Changed the Future: The Ingenious Ideas That Drive Today's Computers*
  John MacCormick – Princeton University Press – 2013

- Microsoft Excel®

- Microsoft Word®

- Adobe® Photoshop

- Adobe® Dreamweaver®

- A Cloud Based Digital Portfolio (e.g. Google Drive)

Free Software Alternatives

- LibreOffice - https://www.libreoffice.org/ (For Excel and Word)

- GIMP - https://www.gimp.org/ (For Photoshop)

- Brackets - http://brackets.io/ (For Dreamweaver)

Unit 1 – The Computer: Basics and Binary

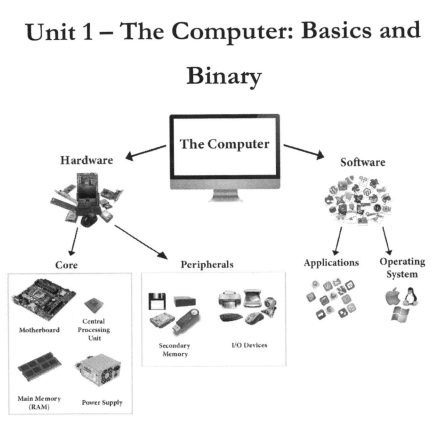

Primary learning outcomes met in this chapter: Abstraction, Global Impact

Computers

If you have ever turned on a phone or surfed the Internet then you have used a computer and should have a basic understanding of what happens when you click the mouse or touch the screen—and how fast it happens! A **computer** is an electronic device that processes data according to a set of instructions or commands, known as a program. Before creating spreadsheets, manipulating images, understanding the Internet, making websites, encrypting data, or learning how to code, it is important to understand the basics of every computer. All computers—desktops, laptops, tablets, and smartphones—convert data into ones and zeros and have the same basic components: software and hardware.

Software

At the lowest level, computer **software** is just a series of ones and zeros. It cannot be touched physically and is usually stored on the computer's hard drive. We can consider software as belonging in two general categories: the operating system and the applications.

Operating System

The **operating system** (OS) includes the desktop, start menu, icons, file view, and common services shared by other programs. It is the visual representation of the computer. Again, at its most basic level, the software is just a series of ones and zeros—usually billions of them at any one time—that cannot be understood by a human, so the operation system helps make these ones and zeros easy to read and understand. Some popular operating systems include Windows 10, MacOS Sierra, and GNU/Linux.

Applications

Pretty much everything else on your computer, except for saved files, is an **application,** including word processors, photo editing software, web browsers, games, and music players. A few popular applications include Microsoft Office, Adobe Photoshop, Apple iTunes, Google Chrome, and Fortnite.

Hardware

The physical parts of the computer are known as **hardware**. These devices—such as the monitor, keyboard, speakers, wires, chips, cables, plugs, disks, printers, mice, and many other items—can be touched. There are two categories of hardware: the **core** and the **peripherals**. The core is made up of the motherboard, the central processing unit (CPU), the main memory, and the power supply. Peripherals consist of the input and output (I/O) devices and the secondary memory.

Core

Everything that happens on a computer goes through the core. Together, the core components—motherboard, CPU, main memory, and power supply—do all the heavy lifting in the computer.

Motherboard

Also called a logic board, a **motherboard** is the standardized printed circuit board that connects the CPU, main memory, and peripherals to each other. Since many different manufacturers make parts for computers, there are a handful of standard form factors to make sure circuits and hardware fit properly. Most motherboards also contain a small integrated chip and firmware, which stores the **BIOS**—or *basic input/output system*—as a way to communicate with the computer (especially before an operating system exists). The **POST** (or power-on self-test) process is also found in this firmware. POST runs basic checks to make sure all core components and peripherals are powering on correctly, usually verified by a chime or series of lights on the motherboard.

Central Processing Unit

The **Central Processing Unit (CPU)** carries out every command or process on the computer. It can be described as the brain of the computer, and it is extremely fast, with a speed that is usually measured in gigahertz—billions of processes per second. By the time information gets to the CPU, it is broken down to ones and zeros. One of the reasons it can process so many commands is because it only needs to recognize these two numbers.

Main Memory

The **main memory** temporarily stores information while it is being sent to the CPU. It also helps break down information to something the CPU can easily understand. Main memory can be thought of as the core's "bouncer." Everything that happens goes through the main memory first. The main memory is often referred to as **RAM**, or **random-access memory**. In other words, information can be retrieved or written to anywhere in the memory. The computer does not have to go through everything stored in the memory to get to the information at the very end. Think about old cassette tapes. To get to the next song, the current song needs to be either played all the way through or fast forwarded through. This kind of memory is called

sequential memory. RAM is more like a CD. To get the next song, just hit next.

Remember, the main memory temporarily holds the information while the CPU processes it. As a result, the more RAM a computer has, the less often it needs to retrieve information and—all other things being equal—the faster it can run programs and the more programs it can run simultaneously.

Power Supply

Just like the power adapter on other electronic devices, a computer's **power supply** converts AC power from the electrical grid to the lower voltage DC power that is needed to power the computer's components. Most power supplies contain a fan to keep them cool and a switch to change between different voltages.

Peripherals

Nearly everything else in the computer is called a **peripheral**, which means it operates at the outside edge of a computer. Peripherals—not the CPU and main memory—are how a user interacts with a computer. Peripherals include the secondary memory, all I/O devices, video or graphics cards, and more.

Secondary Memory

Secondary memory is all memory accessed by the computer, except the main memory. It is used for long-term storage and is physically changed whenever files are saved or deleted. This change makes secondary memory slower than the main memory—although it is still very fast. Secondary memory is much larger than the main memory, and changes are usually only made when a user alters the information stored there, for instance when saving or deleting a file. Common secondary memory devices include hard drives, floppy disks, CD-ROMs, USB storage devices, and flash drives. These peripherals store the software (both OS and applications) that the main memory will access.

I/O Devices

A user interacts with a computer using **input and output (I/O) devices**. Without them, computers would not be very useful. Input devices allow users to send instructions or data to a computer. Keyboards and mice are the most common input devices. They tell the computer when something is typed or clicked. Other input devices include joysticks, microphones, and scanners. Output devices take something from the computer and send it to the user. Monitors and printers are the most common output devices. Others include speakers and virtual reality goggles. Some devices provide both input and output. A touchscreen, for example, takes input when touched and also displays output as a monitor.

Volatile versus Non-volatile

Main memory is usually volatile while secondary memory tends to be non-volatile. The distinction here has to do with the stored information and the power supply. In the case of **volatile** memory, information is lost when the power is turned off whereas with **non-volatile** memory, the information remains. So when you shut down your computer, the main memory is wiped clean, but—thankfully—the secondary memory will remain as is!

Remember that—at its lowest level—a computer only reads zeros and ones. You can think of a computer like a light switch: it is either on or off. When it comes to RAM, a computer can just mark the "switch" on or off, but floppy disks and CD-ROMs work a little differently. Floppy disks are magnetic, and CDs and DVDs use light. A CD has a smooth surface with pits. The smooth parts represent zeros, and the pits stand for ones. In the case of CD-Rs and CD-RWs, the surface becomes reflective when heated to one temperature and non-reflective when heated to another.

The Power of Two

In everyday use, we use a numeral system that uses numerals from zero to nine. So, for every number there are ten different options in each place. As in decagon or decathlon, the prefix *dec-* means ten, so it makes sense that the name of our numeral system starts with *dec-*. The numeral system we ordinarily use is called base-ten, or **decimal,** and it uses ten numerals ranging from zero to nine, which are also called **digits**. In base-two, or **binary,** there are only two numerals used: zero and one, so as in the words bicycle, bifocal, or bipartisan, the prefix *bi-* means two. Each numeral in binary is called a **bit**, which is the smallest unit of information that a computer can process: zero or one, off or on. These bits are so small that it is more practical to group them into bunches of eight, otherwise known as a **byte**.

Each address in memory contains one byte of information, but all but the most rudimentary units of information are larger than one byte, so storing them requires multiple bytes. With today's computers, a byte is an exceedingly small amount of memory, so instead of talking about them in the millions, we use the larger units below. Since the computer only processes zeros and ones, everything is measured in base-two, so one byte is two to the zeroth power, or one. The next unit is the kilobyte, which is two to the tenth power, or 1,024. Notice that it is more than one-thousand bytes—the usual definition of the prefix *kilo-*. A megabyte is 2^{20}, a gigabyte 2^{30}, and a terabyte 2^{40}.

Unit	Actual # of bytes (exponent)	Actual # of bytes (decimal form)	Approximate # of bytes
byte	2^0	1	One
kilobyte	2^{10}	1,024	One-thousand
megabyte	2^{20}	1,048,576	One-million
gigabyte	2^{30}	1,073,741,824	One-billion
terabyte	2^{40}	1,099,511,627,776	One-trillion

Sometimes when companies release hardware, such as hard drives or smartphones, they will consider a megabyte as one-million bytes instead of 2^{20} bytes or a gigabyte as one-billion bytes instead of 2^{30} bytes. If an mp3 player is advertised as having a capacity of twenty gigabytes, the company will put only twenty-billion bytes of memory in it, when twenty gigabytes actually means approximately 21.475 billion bytes. In this case, the customer has been deceived and really bought fewer than 19 GB of storage when they were expecting a full 20 GB.

Converting Binary to Decimal Format

Understanding the base-ten, or decimal, system will make understanding the base-two, or binary, system easier. Binary works in the same exact way as decimal, except that the digits range from zero to one. Therefore, instead of using powers of ten, binary uses powers of two. For example, the first digit is multiplied by 2^0, not 10^0, the second digit is multiplied by 2^1, not 10^1, and so forth. From right to left, the places in the decimal system go 1, 10, 100, 1000... (that is: 10^0, 10^1, 10^2, 10^3...). In binary, they go 1, 2, 4, 8, 16, 32, 64... (that is: 2^0, 2^1, 2^2, 2^3, 2^4, 2^5, 2^6...). Here is an example of a binary number: 1101 0010.

Binary → Decimal

To convert from binary to decimal, simply add the values in binary that are "on" (1 represents on and 0 represents off).

```
1 0 0 1 = 8 + 1 = 9
8 4 2 1
```

$$\underline{1}\ \underline{1}\ \underline{1}\ \underline{1} = 8 + 4 + 2 + 1 = 15$$
$$8\ \ 4\ \ 2\ \ 1$$

$$\underline{0}\quad \underline{1}\quad \underline{0}\quad \underline{1}\quad \underline{1}\quad \underline{1}\quad \underline{0}\quad \underline{0} = 64+16+8+4 = 92$$
$$128\ \ 64\quad 32\ \ 16\quad 8\quad 4\quad 2\quad 1$$

Decimal → Binary

To convert decimal to binary, simply figure out (from left to right) if the binary value needs to be "on" (or a 1). If turning the value on does not make the sum of the number exceed the number, then it should be a 1 (otherwise it is a 0).

$$23\ \rightarrow\ \underline{1}\ \underline{0}\ \underline{1}\ \underline{1}\ \underline{1}\ \rightarrow\ \textit{16 is \textbf{on} since it is less than 23,}$$
$$16\ 8\ 4\ 2\ 1\qquad \textit{8 is \textbf{off} since 16 + 8 is greater than 23}$$

$$46\ \rightarrow\ \underline{1}\quad \underline{0}\ \underline{1}\ \underline{1}\ \underline{1}\ \underline{0}\ \rightarrow\ \textit{32 is \textbf{on} since it is less than 46,}$$
$$32\ 16\ 8\ 4\ 2\ 1\qquad \textit{16 is \textbf{off} since 32 + 16 is greater than 46}$$

$$101\rightarrow\ \underline{1}\quad \underline{1}\quad \underline{0}\ \underline{0}\ \underline{1}\ \underline{0}\ \underline{1}\ \rightarrow\ \textit{64 is \textbf{on} since it is less than 101,}$$
$$64\ 32\ 16\ 8\ 4\ 2\ 1\qquad \textit{32 is \textbf{on} since 64+32 is less than 101}$$

Hexadecimal

Hexadecimal (also known as **base 16**) is a common number system used in computer science. Since there are only ten digits (0-9), the first six letters are used to represent the remaining six characters (a-f). Each character in hexadecimal represents four bits (or a half of a byte). To represent a full byte, two hexadecimal characters are used. These range from **00** (representing 0) to **ff** (representing 255). The chart on the following page shows what each hexadecimal digit represents:

Decimal	Hexadecimal	Binary
0	**0**	0000 0000
1	**1**	0000 0001
2	**2**	0000 0010
3	**3**	0000 0011
4	**4**	0000 0100
5	**5**	0000 0101
6	**6**	0000 0110
7	**7**	0000 0111
8	**8**	0000 1000
9	**9**	0000 1001
10	**a**	0000 1010
11	**b**	0000 1011
12	**c**	0000 1100
13	**d**	0000 1101
14	**e**	0000 1110
15	**f**	0000 1111

When a hexadecimal number is larger than a **nybble** (or half of a byte), the left-most hex digit is worth more, as with any other base. In the decimal number 123, the 3 is worth 3 since it is in the ones place, but the 1 is worth 100 since it is in the one-hundreds place.

Hexadecimal → Binary

To convert a hexadecimal number into binary, look at each nybble individually:

```
d3b → d = 1101, 3 = 0011, b = 1011 → 1101 0011 1011
40f → 4 = 0100, 0 = 0000, f = 1111 → 0100 0000 1111
```

To convert these to decimal, just follow the steps to convert binary to decimal from earlier in this unit.

Binary → Hexadecimal

To convert from binary to hexadecimal, just follow the reverse of above:

```
1001 1100 0001 → 1001 = 9, 1100 = c, 0001 = 1 → 9c1
0110 0011 1110 → 0110 = 6, 0011 = 3, 1110 = e → 63e
```

We have ten fingers, so it makes sense that our society uses base-ten. It makes early counting simple. Since we have all been using base-ten since preschool, we find it easy to work with. Some have argued, however, that **base-eight** or **octal** would be the easiest system to use, especially in computing. Since base-ten uses numerals 0–9, base-eight uses 0–7 (there would be no 8 or 9). These numerals could be eight symbols or emojis, as long as everyone agreed on a standard. For this example, let's stick with 0–7. The ones place (10^0) would still be the ones place (8^0), but the tens place (10^1) would be the eights place (8^1). Every place after that would increase by a power of eight instead of by a power of ten (or a power of two in the case of binary and a power of sixteen in the case of hexadecimal).

Base 8 → Decimal

Converting base-eight is just like converting binary, but instead of the places doubling, they increase by a power of eight:

```
174  →  1   7 4   →  1*64 + 7*8 + 4*1 = 64+56+4 = 114
       64  8 1
520  →  5   2 0   →  5*64 + 2*8 + 0*1 = 64+16+0 = 336
       64  8 1
```

ASCII

ASCII stands for American Standard Code for Information Interchange. Computers can only understand numbers, so letters and symbols must be converted into numbers. This standard provides an agreed-upon protocol to encode other characters as numbers. This includes lowercase letters, uppercase letters, symbols, spaces, tabs, delete, backspace, and more. The first 32 characters (0-31) were used for teletype machines and are now considered obsolete. Most modern character encoding systems, like Unicode, are based on ASCII but allow for the encoding of many more characters, including other alphabets and emojis.

As we've explored in this unit, a computer is a machine, and at its most basic level, it is hardware—a physical thing that you can touch. On its own, hardware isn't useful as much more than a paperweight, but once software—the operating system, programs, and files—are added, it's a different story. Software interacts with hardware as a series of ones and zeros—switches being turned on and off—but these binary numerals can encode text, pictures, sound, video, and the complicated programs that make computers useful to human beings. In the next chapter, we'll turn to one of the most popular and useful of these programs: Adobe Photoshop.

Important Vocabulary

- **Applications** – includes word processors, photo editing software, web browsers, games, music programs, and almost everything else on the computer excluding saved files and the operating system
- **ASCII** – American Standard Code for Information Interchange
- **Binary** – base-two, numeral system that uses zero and one
- **BIOS** – basic input/output system
- **Bit** – each numeral in the binary system, zero or one

- **Byte** – eight bits

- **Central Processing Unit (CPU)** – carries out every command or process on the computer and can be thought of as the brain of the computer

- **Computer** – an electronic device that processes data according to a set of instructions or commands, known as a program

- **Core** – the central processing unit (CPU) and the main memory

- **Decimal** – base-ten, numeral system that uses zero to nine

- **Digit** – each number in the decimal system, zero to nine

- **Hardware** – the physical parts of the computer, including devices such as the monitor, keyboard, speakers, wires, chips, cables, plugs, disks, printers, and mice

- **Hexadecimal** – base 16, number system that uses 0-9 and a–f

- **Input and output (I/O) devices** – how the user interacts with the computer

- **Main memory** – memory that temporarily stores information while it is being sent to the CPU, also called RAM

- **Motherboard** (logic board) – the standardized printed circuit board that connects the CPU, main memory, and peripherals

- **Nonvolatile** – does not need a power supply. Information is physically written to the device

- **Nybble (or Nibble)** – half byte, four bits

- **Operating System** – the visual representation of the computer

- **Peripherals** – the input and output (I/O) devices and the secondary memory

- **POST** – power-on self-test

- **Power Supply** – converts AC electricity to the lower voltage DC electricity that is needed to power the computer

- **Random Access Memory (RAM)** – memory that can be retrieved or written to anywhere without having to go through all the previous memory

- **Secondary Memory** – used for long term storage and is physically changed when files are saved or deleted

- **Sequential memory** – memory used to store back-up data on a tape

- **Volatile** – needs a power supply. Turning off the power deletes information

- **Software** – includes the operating system and the applications. It is usually stored on a computer's hard drive and cannot physically be touched. At the lowest level, it is a series of ones and zeros

Suggested Reading

- "Digital Explosion." *Blown to Bits.* Chapter 1. Pages 1-17

- "Introduction." *Nine Algorithms that Changed the Future.* Chapter 1. Pages 7-12

Unit 2 – Photo Editing and Adobe Photoshop

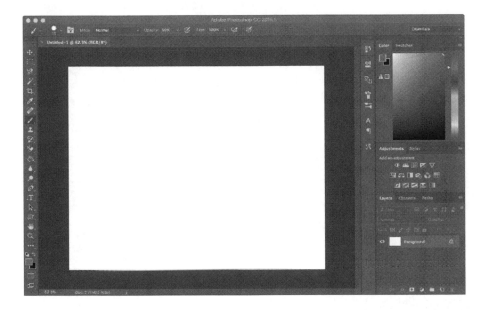

Primary learning outcome met in this chapter: Creativity

Introduction to Adobe Photoshop

The ability for anyone with a personal computer to easily and convincingly manipulate images may be one of the most significant changes of the last several decades. First published in 1990, Adobe Photoshop is considered to be the industry standard graphics editor and is the current market leader for commercial bitmap and image manipulation. Along with Adobe Acrobat, it is one of the most well-known pieces of software produced by Adobe Systems. It is used in most—if not all—jobs related to the use of visual elements and is usually simply referred to as "Photoshop." Indeed, this program is so ubiquitous that its name is oftentimes used as verb, so you can "photoshop" a picture just as you would xerox a document or google who played Willow on *Buffy the Vampire Slayer* (although Adobe Systems would prefer that you didn't).

With Photoshop, a user can create and modify digital images, or rather, images in electronic form. Photoshop allows users to create original artwork, modify or combine existing pictures, add text or special effects to a webpage, and restore or touch up old photographs, among other tasks. The images to be modified can come from many places, including the web, digital cameras, or scanners. Once created or imported, the artwork can be modified. Users can rotate or resize these images. They can add text or change colors, and they can combine these images with other pictures. Users make such changes by modifying the **pixels** — the tiny dots that each represent a certain color. More pixels means higher resolution but also larger files.

When the image is ready to be saved, there are many possible file types to choose from. The most common are **.psd**, **.png**, **.jpg**, and **.gif**. Photoshop's native file format is **.psd**, which will be larger than the others. Other applications will not usually be able to read this format. Most applications can read the other three file types, which are also significantly smaller in size than the Photoshop format.

When modifying images in Photoshop, it's always a good idea to keep a copy of the original image in case you need to reuse the image or correct a mistake. To make sure the original image remains unaltered, use the *Save as...* command as soon as the image has been opened then choose a different name for the image that is going to be modified. This will create a copy of the original that will remain untouched and can be opened if there is ever a need to start from scratch.

The Workspace

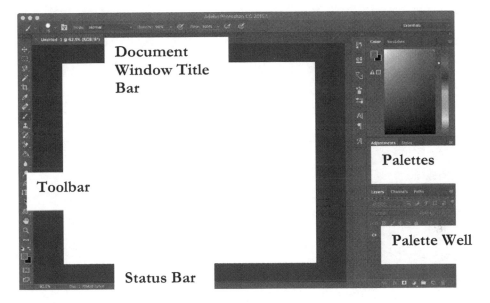

The **workspace** is the area between the tool option bar and the status bar. The workspace includes all the palettes, the toolbar, and the open document windows.

The **title bar** contains the name of the program as well as the close, minimize, and maximize buttons.

The **tool options bar** is located under the menu bar and shows more options for the selected tool from the toolbox. When a new tool is selected, the tool option bar will change to accommodate the selected tools. This option bar contains very useful additions to the selected tool that vary from tool to tool.

The **palettes** are small windows which start stacked up on the right side of the workspace. These palettes may be moved anywhere in the workspace and reordered as desired. The most useful palettes are the history palette and the layer palette, which show the last twenty actions performed and information about each layer in the image respectively.

Located at the bottom of the screen, the **status bar** displays information about the file size and the active tool.

Layers

A layer is a part of the image that can be modified independently. They work like anatomy books that use clear pages to show the different systems of the body. Each page can be folded back to show what the layer underneath looks like. Photoshop supports up to 8000 layers. Since the images that are blocked by other layers are still there, layers can make the file size very large. The image can be flattened to decrease the file size. Flattening an image discards all the image information that cannot be seen or that is blocked. Most formats other than .psd do not support layers, so saving in these formats will automatically flatten the image.

The **layer palette** shows the active layer by highlighting it. Multiple layers can be selected by holding down *shift* or *control/command*. To make layers easier to see, individual layers can be hidden. To do this, click the eye icon to the left of the layer. Clicking the empty box where the eye used to be will make the layer visible again. Changing the layer's opacity to 0% from the top of the layer palette will achieve the same effect.

The **toolbox** contains frequently used Photoshop commands. Each tool is marked by a graphical representation of what the tool does. When the user moves the pointer over a tool, a screen tip will appear stating the name of the tool and the keyboard shortcut in parentheses. Some tools have other tools hidden behind them, denoted by a small triangle at the bottom right hand corner of the tool. To see the hidden tools, hold down the pointer on the tool or right click.

Move Tool

Marquee Tools

Lasso Tools

Magic Wand Tool

Crop Tool

Healing Brush/Patch Tool

Paint Brush/
Pencil Tools

Clone Tool

Eraser Tools

Paint Bucket/Gradient Tools

Blur/Sharpen/Smudge

Dodge/Burn/Sponge Tools

Pen Tool

Type Tools

Hand Tool

Zoom Tool

Set Background/
Foreground Colors

Selecting

When editing or combining images, you may need to take one piece of the image and either move or edit it. Photoshop offers many ways to select parts of images, including the *marquee tool*, the *magic wand*, and three types of *lasso tools*.

The **marquee tool**, which has rectangular and elliptical options, should be used when the object is either a rectangular or round shape.

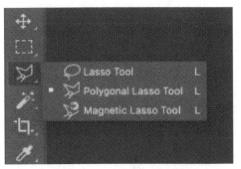

The **magic wand** can be used when the background is significantly different from the image. This tool automatically detects changes in color, so it is useful when an object is on a solid colored background. For other irregular shapes, the best way to select them is to use the lasso tools.

The three lasso tools are regular, polygonal, and magnetic. The **regular lasso** tool should be used for tracing the entire image by hand. When an object's edges are all straight, use the **polygonal lasso**. Like the magic wand tool, the **magnetic lasso** automatically detects changes in color. To use this tool, trace the object roughly, and the lasso will set anchors along the edges of the image.

In the tool option bar for each of these tools, there are three useful options for making selections. The **new selection** tool is used when starting from scratch. The **add to selection** tool is used when a part is missing from the original selection or when another object needs to be added. The **subtract from selection** tool is used to remove part of the selection from the object.

There are also useful options in the **select** menu under the menu bar: **all, deselect**, and **inverse**. *All* selects the whole layer, *deselect* gets rid of any selections on the page, and *inverse* switches what is selected and unselected so that anything selected becomes unselected and anything unselected becomes selected. The *modify* option under this menu contains other useful options, which allow the selection to be expanded or contracted.

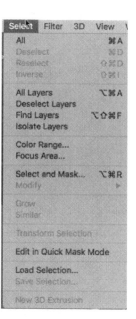

Now that an object has been selected, use the **move** tool to drag the selection from one image to another or to move it within the same image. If the move tool is not selected, then dragging the selection will only move the marquee or the dotted line, not the image selection itself. Right clicking inside the selection also allows for a new layer to be created from the selection, either by copying or cutting the selection.

Layer Masks

Another way to select part of an image is to erase everything else. It can be hard to restore the deleted portion, however, if an error is made. The solution to this problem is masks. Masks allow you to crop out parts of a  picture without modifying the pixels, so if a mistake is made, you can easily fix it by changing the mask, not the picture itself.

If a layer is locked as a background, double the click the layer in the layer palette, name it, and click ok to create a new layer. To begin masking, click the *mask button* that looks like a square with a circle cut out at the bottom of the layer palette. You can also go to the *layer menu* and select *layer mask* and *reveal all*. Once a mask is on the layer, it can be effectively erased by painting the mask black.

Alternately, you can achieve the opposite effect by painting the mask white. It is important to set the paint brush being used to 100% hardness in order to create a perfect edge. Otherwise, the picture will appear to have a glowing edge. While using masks, use the *zoom tool* to get closer to the pixel level to get a crisp edge. Holding down *shift* and clicking with the paint brush will cause the dots to connect in a straight line, making the edges much crisper. See the list of useful shortcuts at the end of this unit.

Master Copy

Once an image has been masked, it is a good idea to duplicate this layer and lock the original as a master copy. If mistakes are made that cannot be reversed then a new duplicate can be made from the master copy. One way to create a duplicate of the masked layer is to hold down the *ctrl* key and click on the thumbnail of the mask. This selects the white area of the mask. Next make sure the thumbnail of the image is selected and select *Layer... New... Layer via Copy* from the menu bar. Double click the name of the original copy, rename it "master," then click the padlock icon at the top of the layer palette. Now that the master copy is locked, turn off the layer's visibility and drag it to the bottom of the layer palette.

Transforming

Transformations are a way to scale, skew, distort, warp, flip, rotate, and shift the perspective on a layer. The most useful of these is scale. Scaling up usually does not work well since the layer can become pixilated. To scale down a layer select *Edit... Transform... Scale*, or use the keyboard shortcut for free transform: *ctrl/command + t*. To ensure that the dimensions of the layer do not get distorted, hold down *shift* and grab the layer by a corner. When the transformation is complete, press *enter* to accept the changes or *esc* to cancel the transformation.

Filters

Filters are a way to edit an image's pixels to create a desired look or feel. There are several filters

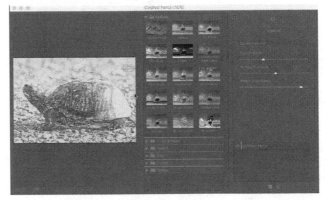

built in to Photoshop. A downside of filters is that they do change the pixels, so the only way to remove a filter is to undo or step backwards, but by applying a smart filter to a layer, the information in the original layer will be stored so that the filter can be removed or changed easily. If a smart filter was not applied then there will be no way to recover the original image once the file has been saved and closed. Categories of filters include **artistic filters, stylize filters, render filters, noise filters, blur filters,** and **sketch filters**. All the filters can be seen by selecting the *filter* menu in the menu bar. Each category of filter includes many actual filters, such as **colored pencil, smudge stick, watercolor, pinch, ripple, wave, gaussian blur, tiles, clouds,** and **glowing edges**. Most of these filters have sub-menus as well that are indicated with an ellipsis. To see most categories at the same time select *Filter Gallery....*

Layer Styles

Layer styles are a good way to add effects to a layer. Unlike filters, layer styles can be turned on or off and changed as needed, even if the file has been saved and closed. Most of the options in layer styles affect the edge of the layer, so if a layer takes up the whole canvas, then layer styles might not be the best choice. A few useful styles are the **drop shadow, outer glow, bevel and emboss,** and **stroke**. To bring up the layer styles window, double click to the right of the layer name on the layer palette or select *Layer... Layer Styles* from the menu bar. The check boxes can turn the styles on and off, and more options can be seen by clicking on the name of the style.

Gradients

A gradient is a fill in which two or more colors blend together. The default gradient colors are the current foreground and background, but infinite possibilities can be selected by clicking on the preview of the gradient in the tool option bar. Gradients can also use transparency to achieve certain effects. In addition to colors, there are also five different types of gradients: linear, radial, angle, reflected, and diamond.

Type

The type tool allows users to add text to Photoshop to help get a message across to an audience. Examples include magazine and newspaper advertisements. In such advertisements, many different fonts and colors can be used to emphasize certain parts of the overall image. In most cases, text or type should be used sparingly in Photoshop, as the overall file should mostly be the image itself. Type reinforces or complements the existing image. The text should be direct and large enough to be easily seen without being so large as to detract from the image itself.

Font Families

There are three main font families: **serif, sans serif**, and **symbols**. A *serif* is a tail, or stoke, at the end of a character, and the word *sans* translates to "without." In other words, serif fonts contain a tail or stroke on most characters while sans serif fonts do not. Symbols are unique characters such as $, #, &, @, and *.

Editing Fonts

When the type tool is used, it automatically adds a new layer to the file. Simply click and type to add text. To change the size, color, or font of the text, highlight the text and change these things in the tool option bar at the top of the window. Selecting all the text in a layer can be done by double clicking on the thumbnail of the text layer in the layer palette. For more options to adjust the font, such as tracking or kerning, use the character palette, which looks like an A with a vertical bar to the right when collapsed. Many characteristics of fonts can be changed. One aspect that can be modified is the type spacing or the space in between each character. The type spacing can be set to monotype or proportional spacing. Monotype makes every character take up the same amount of space (i would take up the same amount of space as w). With proportional spacing, each letter takes up a different amount of space depending on the letter (this book uses proportional spacing!).

In this chapter, we've had a chance to start working with a program that is indispensable to many creative people. Photographers, graphic designers, magazine editors, and many, many other professionals use Photoshop every day in their careers. By mastering the tasks introduced above, you'll be well on your way to acquiring a set of skills with virtually unlimited potential. In the next unit, you will have a chance to begin learning Microsoft Excel, a program that almost anyone who has ever worked in an office will be familiar with. Making spreadsheets may not be as exciting as working with pictures, but gaining familiarity with this surprisingly powerful application will prepare you for an even more surprising number of jobs.

Shortcuts

Ctrl + N:	New document
Ctrl + O:	Open document
Ctrl + S:	Save
Ctrl + A:	Select All
Ctrl + D:	Deselect
Ctrl + Z:	Undo
Ctrl + Alt + Z:	Step Backwards (Undo more than 1 step)
Ctrl + Shift + Z:	Step Forward (Redo more than one step)
Alt + Mouse Scroll:	Zoom in/out
Space Bar:	Hand tool (move around zoomed picture)
V:	Move tool
B:	Brush tool
G:	Paint Bucket/Gradient Tool
E:	Eraser
T:	Type Tool
M:	Marquee tools (rectangular, elliptical)
L:	Lasso tools (free lasso, polygonal, magnetic)
W:	Magic wand tool
D:	Set foreground/background to black/white
X:	Flip foreground and background color
[:	Make brush one size smaller
] :	Make brush one size larger
Shift + click:	Paint/draw straight lines
Ctrl + J:	New layer via copy
Ctrl + Click:	Select contents of the layer
(on layer thumbnail)	(white part of masks)

Unit 3 – Spreadsheets and Microsoft Excel

Primary learning outcome met in this chapter: Data and Information

Introduction to Microsoft Excel

Prior to the introduction of electronic spreadsheets, accounting and bookkeeping had to be done by hand on paper—a slow and laborious process. With the introduction of VisiCalc on the Apple II (in 1979)

and Lotus 1-2-3 on the IBM PC (in 1983), these tasks quickly became computerized. Since then, the use of spreadsheets has spread well beyond financial record keeping. Microsoft Excel gradually supplanted Lotus 1-2-3 and—with the release of version five in 1993—became the overwhelmingly dominant spreadsheet application. The program features an intuitive interface and graphing tools and is capable of a high level of calculation. These features—along with aggressive marketing and its bundling as part of Microsoft Office—have made Excel one of the most popular computer applications to date.

A spreadsheet is basically a grid used to store information, usually numbers. This grid consists of rows and columns. **Rows** go from left to right like rows of seats in a movie theater and are labeled using numbers starting at one. In Excel, there are over one million possible rows. **Columns** go from top to bottom like the columns that used to hold up Greek ruins. Columns are labeled using letters starting with A. When more than 26 columns are present, double letters are used, continuing with AA, AB, AC, AD, etc., then triple letters starting with AAA, AAB… all the way until XFD.

Each individual piece of the grid—where the rows and columns intersect—is called a **cell**. Each cell is labelled with the column letter followed by the row number so that A1 is the cell at the top left of the spreadsheet. Three basic items can be placed into the cells: labels, constants, and formulas. A **label** is text that describes some part of the spreadsheet, such as a name or amount. Labels are not meant for the computer but rather for humans to better understand the information in the cell. A **constant** is any number that the user enters into the spreadsheet. It will not change unless the user changes it manually. A **formula** is an equation that can perform calculations on existing cells. All formulas must start with an equals sign. Examples of formulas are: *=5 + 6*5* or *=2*F4 - A7*. Notice that F4 and A7 are cells, so whatever numbers are in these cell will be subtracted or multiplied. If this cell contains a label or has been left blank then errors may occur.

Functions

Excel has many built-in functions that can help manipulate data. Some of these functions include finding minimums or maximums, calculating averages or sums, performing trig functions, and carrying out conditional statements. There are more than two-hundred functions in Excel. They can be found either by knowing the name of the function or by going to *Formulas… Insert Function…* A list of functions will then pop-up that can be narrowed down by searching or selecting a category. Notice that all functions (like formulas) begin with an equals sign.

At the bottom of the window, there will be a brief description on what the function does. A more detailed description will be given when the function is selected.

The following chart shows some useful functions and how they look when entered into the cell:

Name	Description	Sample Code	Appears in Cell
AVG	Finds the average from a list of numbers	=AVG(A1, A4, A6, A8)	4.75
MIN & *MAX*	Finds the minimum/maximum value of a list of numbers and returns that number	=MIN(D1:D9) = MAX(B13:B23)	37 104
COUNT & *COUNTA*	Counts how many cells have numerical data. CountA counts all data, text included	=COUNT(A1:K30) =COUNTA(A1:K30)	29 46
SUM	Adds up all the values and returns the answer	=SUM(A1,A5,B3,D5)	73
IF	This can return different things depending on whether the condition is met. The first item after the condition is displayed if it is true and the second if false	=IF(B1<C1,"You win", "You lose")	You lose

Embedding Functions

Functions and formulas can work together. Some functions can even be embedded—or inserted—into other functions. For example, if you wanted to find what group of cells had the highest average, then you might write it like this:

=max(average(A1:A20), average(B1:B20), average(C1:C20))

Formatting

Formatting is a way to make the data in a spreadsheet more visually appealing. This can be done by changing the look of numbers; altering the font, color, or size; adding borders; or aligning the text in different ways. By right clicking on a cell, or selecting *Formatting... Format Cells...* under the *Home* tab, the *format cells* window will appear. There will be six tabs to choose from at the top of this window. These tabs can easily be mastered by experimenting with the different options.

Conditional Formatting

Excel has some built-in formatting tools that will automatically perform calculations for the user. Some of these tools can highlight cells that meet specific criteria, such as equaling a value, being greater than a certain value, or being less than a certain value. Other tools can highlight cells that are in the top or bottom five or ten or that have any given value. It can also be done with percentages. Conditional formatting can also turn cells into mini graphs using data bars or different color schemes. These graphs are determined by the highest and lowest values and can be modified by going into *more options*.

To remove conditional formatting, highlight the cells and select *Clear Rules* in the conditional formatting menu.

Auto Formatting

Excel includes several pre-made templates that can change a spreadsheet's look automatically, eliminating the need to change colors and borders by hand. To use a template, select the cells that are to be formatted, then select *Formatting... Format as Table...* from the *Home* menu bar.

Charts

Excel can also create charts and graphs from the data in a spreadsheet. There are several different charts that can be created, the most common being the bar, pie, and line charts. Under each chart type, there are sub-types that can give the graph more effects, such as making it three-dimensional or showing relationships throughout the data. Remember that a line graph shows change over time. To choose the desired type of chart, select it under the *Insert* tab.

Before a chart type is selected, the data range needs to be chosen. This can be done by highlighting the cells that contain the data. To select cells that are not adjacent, choose the first set of cells, then hold down the *ctrl* key and select the next set. Once you have selected the data, click on the type of chart as shown in the picture above. The *Design, Layout,* and *Format* tabs that will appear when you click on the chart can be used to add titles as well as axes names, legends, and data labels. Some of these tabs are shown below.

Printing

There are many options for printing an Excel document. These options can all be found under *File... Page Setup...*

Under the *Page* tab, the orientation of the page can be set (either vertical or horizontal). The spreadsheet may also be scaled to fit on a desired number of pages. Another useful tab is the *Sheet* tab. The most useful item under this tab is the *Gridlines* checkbox under the *Print* section. When checked, this tab will display the lines in the spreadsheet. Excel does not show gridlines by default.

Spreadsheet applications are essential tools for organizing and calculating. As the most popular of these programs, Excel is ubiquitous in offices around the world. Spreadsheets make calculating budgets, organizing large events, or managing groups of people much more manageable. Mastering the powerful features of Excel will serve you well in an enormous variety of careers. In the next chapter, we will move on to a less visible but unavoidable part of modern computing: compression.

Unit 4 – Data and Compression

Primary learning outcome met in this chapter: Data and Information

Why Compress Data?

Today's world is filled with endless audio, images, videos, apps, and more. These files are being saved, sent, and downloaded more than ever before. Hard drive sizes may be increasing, but uncompressed files will still fill them up quickly. For example, an uncompressed, 90-minute, HD (1080p) movie takes up approximately one terabyte of hard drive space. A common compression format for video called H.264 allows the same 90-minute HD movie to be stored using only 65 gigabytes, 15 times smaller than the uncompressed version. By using a video space calculator, it is easy to see how different formats (or number of frames per second) can result in dramatically different file sizes.

And that's just referring to space on a personal hard drive. Today, most of this digital information is sent over the Internet (more on that in unit five). The larger the file size, the longer it takes to download. Or even worse, streaming movies and TV shows may suffer from poor image quality or buffering! With the amount of data sent over the internet every second, it is important to keep file sizes small without compromising the quality of the material.

Heuristic Approach

In programming, a **heuristic approach** is an approach that gives results that are "good enough" when an exact answer is not necessary. This is seen in the famous "traveling salesman problem," which tries to map out the shortest distance between many cities. The problem is simple with only a few cities, but it becomes exponentially more difficult as more cities are added. This problem is **computationally hard**, meaning even a computer would take too long to find the exact solution. An instance using 85,900 "cities" was solved in 2006, but it took the equivalent of a computer running 24 hours a day for 136 years. The amount of time and computational power to find this solution was out of proportion to the result. It would have been more sensible to find a "good" route in a much shorter amount of time.

A heuristic approach is also appropriate when compressing data. The "good enough" solution in compression is determined by the relationship between size and quality. To keep text, images, audio, video, etc. from losing any quality, the size of the compressed file will not be much smaller than the original. When compressing a song (as when turning it into an mp3), a heuristic approach would be to take out enough of the data to substantially reduce the file size while keeping the sound quality high when played back on a personal speaker.

Lossy vs. Lossless

When compressing data, a heuristic approach may be the right choice. If a smaller size is more important than quality, it's okay to lose some data. When date is lost during compression, it is known as **lossy** compression. Ideally, the human eye or ear will not be able to detect this loss of data. For example, the human eye cannot see the difference between very similar shades of red, so when compressing an image, the computer may look at colors that are very similar and change them all to the same color. When dealing with millions of colors, this simplification could greatly reduce the file size, allowing it to load faster on websites or to be sent faster through email. For an audio file, this might mean a reduction in the **sample rate** or **bits per second**. An audio file could be reduced from 96 kHz to 44.1 kHz without the human ear being able to notice enough difference to justify the much larger file size.

In situations where an uncompressed file needs to maintain all the original information it had before it was compressed then it is important to get the exact solution. When compressing text files or emails, for example, it is necessary to maintain all the original information, otherwise certain letters or words might be missing. This kind of compression is known as **lossless** compression, as it does not lose any data during compression.

Metadata

On its own, data itself may not be useful. Additional information about the data is needed. This "data about the data" is known as **metadata**. Even though the Greek prefix *meta-* means "after," it usually comes at the very beginning of the file. Most file types require metadata and have a strict set of rules about where it is located and how long it needs to be. Metadata may include title, author, keywords, date created, location where it was created, file size, height, width, and so on. Examples of what this metadata could look like will be discussed later in this chapter.

Text Compression

Given the rapidly falling costs of storage and bandwidth, large file sizes might not seem like a big deal, but as we will see in unit five, smaller file sizes are crucial when sending information thousands of miles over the Internet. Images, audio files, and videos are much larger than text files, generally speaking, but with the sheer number of emails and text messages sent every day, text compression is just as important. When compressing text, however, it is critical that no data are lost. Losing 10% of an email might make it unreadable, so text compression will always be **lossless**.

An easy way to think about text compression is by looking at common words or patterns of letters and representing them with a single character or letter. Let's assume that every time the word "and" appeared in this book, it was replaced with a plus sign. The word "and" appears approximately 780 times in this book, taking up 2340 characters. If each "and" was replaced with a plus sign, it would take up only 780 characters. If the spaces before and after the word are included (_and_) that represents 3900 characters. Using a plus sign could reduce this to only take 780 characters (plus six characters of metadata to tell the next user that the file was compressed). Imagine if other common words or letter groupings were changed into symbols. The letters "th" appear almost 4500 times in this book. Just by swapping "and" and "th" for symbols, we can reduce the length of this book by almost 8500 characters. That is more than five full pages! Without **metadata** explaining what words or letter groups were swapped, however, this would all be useless.

Compressing Text Example

♣	**wood**	How much ♣ ♠a ♥ ♦ if a ♥ ♠ ♦ ♣?
♦	**chuck**	
♥	♣ ♦	By following the key (or metadata) to the left, the message can be uncompressed to read:
♠	**could**	

IIow much wood could a woodchuck chuck if a woodchuck could chuck wood?

The original message contains 58 characters and the compressed message contains 20 characters in the message and 20 characters in the key (metadata). This might not seem like much, but this simple compression made the file about 30% smaller. Imagine taking that uncompressed HD movie from the beginning of this chapter and making it 30% smaller. The original file was a terabyte, so this would save about 300 gigabytes. Obviously, video cannot be compressed in exactly this manner, but there are even more ways to compress video to make it much smaller than the original. But think of how much text is on a computer: Word documents, emails, and more. If everyone tried to send dozens of uncompressed emails every day, Internet speeds would be at risk. This will be discussed in the next unit.

Image Compression

A **pixel**, short for picture element, is the basic unit of color on a computer display. The size of pixels on a screen can change depending on the resolution of the display. A larger number of pixels on a display requires a smaller pixel size, resulting in a better quality image. Scanning a picture into a computer or taking a digital photo turns an image into millions of individual pixels. In order for the computer to understand them, these pixels are represented as binary numbers. Large pixels can make an image look blocky, a phenomenon known as **pixelation**. Contrary to what you may have seen in movies, there is no way to "enhance" these images since they do not contain the binary information for the missing pixels.

Black and White Images

A simple example of converting binary code to a black and white image will help clarify how ones and zeros can become an image on a monitor. Black and white work well for this example, since they can be represented by a single bit. 0 = black, 1 = white. In addition to the color data, there must also be metadata to indicate such things as height and width.

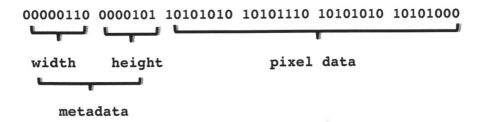

In this example, the metadata are two bytes (16 bits) long and represent width and height, one byte for each. This kind of information is predetermined by the file type, and every file of this type must follow the same rules. If the first byte is converted from binary, it equals 6, and  the height is 5. So, this image is 6 pixels by 5 pixels. The remaining 4 bytes of this file represent each pixel's color, black or white. Just like reading, start at the top left and fill in the appropriate colors. "1s" will be black and "0s" will be white. Continue to the next row when needed. The result will say "Hi".

Color Images and RGB Values

There are two main color models to consider: CMYK and RGB.
CMYK is used for printing and stands for **c**yan, **m**agenta, **y**ellow, and black (**k**ey), where the number associated with each letter is the percentage of each color used. This color model is subtractive, meaning white is the color of the paper and black is the combination of all the colors. Most printers have a separate black ink cartridge since it is more cost effective than combining the other three colors and replacing them more often.

RGB (which stands for **r**ed, **g**reen, and **b**lue) refers to the color of light used in most monitors or screens and is an additive color model. This means that no light is black and the combination of all light is white. Instead of using a percentage from 0–100, RGB uses one byte (2^8 or 0–255) to represent each color. Since there are three colors, each RGB value (1 pixel) is 3 bytes of data (24 bits), much larger than the single bit each pixel in a black and white image uses. If the RGB value of a color is (255, 0, 0), all the red light is on and no green or blue light is on, so it would be a red light. Likewise, (0, 0, 255) would be blue. Using 24 bits to represent color gives 2^{24} possible combinations, that is 16,777,216 colors.

One way that color images can be compressed is by grouping colors that are very similar to one another. When there are almost 17 million colors, a color and another color only a few bits away from it will look identical to the human eye, so compression algorithms for images take these similar colors and save them all as the same color. Most of the time this simplification should not change the quality of the image, but when these algorithms are too aggressive, color banding occurs, which can be seen in the image below.

The modern world generates an enormous amount of information, and we don't just store this data, we move it around, oftentimes from one side of the planet to the other. Without compression, storing and moving all this information would be prohibitively expensive if not impossible. Compression, then, is one of the foundations of modern computing, and by gaining an understanding of the basics of compression, you have taken another step toward understanding how computers work—and work together—today. In the following unit, we'll go further down this path by discussing the networks that connect computers to each other, especially the network of networks that is foundational not just to computer science but to modern life: the Internet.

Important Vocabulary

- **Computationally hard** – a problem that takes too long even for a computer to find the exact solution

- **Heuristic approach** – an approach that gives results that are "good enough" when an exact answer is not necessary

- **Lossless** – data compression that does not lose data during compression

- **Lossy** – data compression that loses data during compression

- **Bit Rate** – the number of bits that can be processed per second

- **Sample Rate** – how often an analog signal is used when converting to digital, usually measured in bits per second

- **Metadata** – additional data about the main data, usually at the beginning of a file

- **Pixelation** – when individual pixels are too large and the image begins to look blocky

- **CMYK** – color model used for printing. Stands for cyan, magenta, yellow, and black (key), where the number associated with each letter is the percentage of each color used

- **RGB** – color model used for most monitors or screens. Stands for red, green, and blue, referring to the color of light

Suggested Reading

- "Naked in the Sunlight." *Blown to Bits*. Chapter 2. Pages 19-72

- "Ghosts in the Machine." *Blown to Bits*. Chapter 3. Pages 73-108

- "Data Compression." *Nine Algorithms that Changed the Future*. Chapter 7. Pages 78-89

Unit 5 – The Internet

Primary learning outcomes met in this chapter: The Internet, Abstraction

Origins

On its own, a computer is a useful tool, but when connected to other computers, its potential increases exponentially. As consequential as the introduction of personal computers was, its impact on society was not as significant as the introduction of many other technologies, such as the telephone, radio, or the automobile. This changed with the rise of the Internet. Is there any aspect of modern life that has not been altered by the Internet?

A computer **network** is a group of computers that are connected so they can share resources using a data link—either a cable or wireless connection. Networks can vary in size from a large business with thousands of computers that are all sharing files to a school with twenty computers to a family with three computers all connecting to the same home media server. The **Internet** is a network of these smaller networks connected according to a specific set of rules that computers use to facilitate their communications with each other. These rules are called **protocols** and the one the Internet uses is aptly named **Internet Protocol** (**IP**), which works closely with Transmission Control Protocol (**TCP**).

The Internet is not as new as it may seem. Its origins date to 1969 and the Advanced Research Projects Agency Network (**ARPANET**). This was the first network to use the TCP/IP protocols that are still used today (but they did not become the standard until 1982). ARPANET broke data up into smaller, more manageable pieces called **packets,** which continue to be the basis for digital communication today. Even though it was decommissioned on February 28, 1990, ARPANET is still considered the foundation of today's Internet.

IP Addresses

Every business and home has a unique address, so the post office can deliver mail. Similarly, every computer and connected device have their own address, known as an Internet Protocol address or **IP address** for short. Even though everything on the computer is stored in binary, IP addresses are usually written in a form that humans can understand, like telephone numbers. Since every computer, printer, router, smartphone, and assorted device is connected to the Internet, the number of IP addresses are growing fast. These are all managed by the Internet Assigned Number Authority (**IANA**), a non-profit organization which is a department of the Internet Corporation for Assigned Names and Numbers (**ICANN**).

IPv4 vs. IPv6

Internet Protocol has gone through many versions, but the fourth version (IPv4) routes the most Internet traffic. IPv4 uses 32-bit addresses, which allow for a possible 2^{32} or 4,294,967,296 possible addresses. These addresses are broken down into 4 bytes, each separated by a period and displayed in decimal, giving a value from 0-255. An IPv4 address looks something like: **34.203.4.189**.

Four billion IP addresses seemed like more than enough back in the early 1980s when IPv4 was created, but with so many people on the Internet using multiple devices today, they have run out. In the late 1990s the Internet Engineering Task Force (**IETF**) came up with an addressing system that used 128-bits called IPv6. This allows fo 2^{128} possible addresses, that is more than 3.4×10^{38} possibilities. This is an extremely large number, much larger than the number of grains of sand or even the number of atoms on the planet. There will never be close to that many addresses. Since writing these addresses in bits require 128 ones and zeros, they are written in hexadecimal and might look like this: **2001:0db8:85a3:0000:0000:8a2e:0370:7334**. Since there are so many unused bytes, zeros can be omitted and replaced with a double colon: **2001:0db8:85a3::8a2e:0370:7334**. Most sites have both an IPv4 and IPv6 address to prepare for a smooth transition to using only IPv6, something that most people won't even notice when it happens.

MAC Addresses

Since IP addresses are stored in software, they can change and be deleted. For this reason, all devices that are connected to a network also have a unique, physical address that is stored in the computer's ROM. This address is called the media access control address, or MAC address for short. Since they are physically added by the manufacturer, a MAC address can also indicate what brand of device is attached to the address.

The Web

People commonly refer to the Internet as the World Wide Web—or simply the **Web**. Although the Web is part of the Internet, they are not the same thing. The Internet has many services, each using separate protocols. The Web is just one of them. Other services and protocols include email (Internet Message Access Protocol or **IMAP** and Post Office Protocol or **POP**), Internet telephony (Voice over Internet or **VoIP**), and file transfer (**FTP**). The web displays websites on web browsers and uses Hypertext Transfer Protocol (**HTTP**) or Hypertext Transfer Protocol Secure (**HTTPS**), which has extra security like **SSL/TLS** (more in unit seven). Therefore, website names always begin with *http://* or *https://* (sometime the browser hides this, but it is there).

HTML

Hyper Text Markup Language or **HTML** is the standard for creating web pages, hence the name of the protocol web pages use: Hyper Text Transfer Protocol. A markup language is just a way to format text so that it stands out—changing colors, fonts, alignment, etc. It is not a programming language. HTML uses tags that are between angle brackets (< and >) and is usually paired with **Cascading Style Sheets** (**CSS**) and **JavaScript**. We will return to HTML and CSS in unit six and JavaScript in unit eight.

Addressing

A website is made up of files stored on a computer, also called a **server**. A server could be a home computer, part of a large server farm, or anything in between. When a computer requests a specific file (like a website) or service from a server, it is known as the **client**. The Internet runs on this **client-server model**. A client sends a request to a server then the server sends the requested information back to the client. The client can request the server by using its unique IP address (IPv4 or IPv6). It would be very tedious to memorize every IP address of every webpage, so instead, domain names are used.

A **domain name** is simply a name given or linked to an IP address. These are the website names that are typed into the web browser, like *www.google.com* or *wordpress.org*. Google's IP address is 8.8.8.8 (not that hard to remember) and WordPress's is 74.200.243.254 (among others). Besides the home page, most websites contain many other pages or files. These files and folders use a Uniform Resource Locator or **URL** to call or locate specific files from the domain. An example of a URL is *https://www.youtube.com/watch?v=dQw4w9WgXcQ*. The domain name of this file is *youtube.com*. When a domain name is used on its own, the URL will usually default to opening a file called *index.html* or *home.html*, so by entering the domain name *https://www.mrhare.gov* into your browser's address bar will cause it to open the URL *https://www.mrhare.gov/index.html*. Any domain can also be preceded by a **subdomain**, so pages like https://*csprinciples.mrhare.gov* or *https://awesomeness.mrhare.gov* are still owned by *https://www.mrhare.gov*.

DNS

When a client requests a file from a server, the first thing the client needs to do is to determine the IP address of the URL's domain name. This process is kicked off by the Domain Name System (**DNS**). The DNS is one of the smaller networks that make up the Internet and contains many servers that act like phone books. These computers are called **name servers** and contain many IP addresses and their matching domain names. Most of these name servers are owned by Internet Service Providers (**ISPs**), such as Comcast, AT&T, Time Warner, Verizon, Cox, and others. If the first name server does not contain the requested domain's IP address, it will ask another name server for it. If that name server does not know it, it will ask another name server. This process will continue until the IP address is found and sent back through the name servers to the client.

Since there are so many IP addresses and domain names, most name servers only contain a small portion of them. But, there are thirteen **Root Name Servers** that contain every single domain name and IP address in the world. Most of the root name servers are networks of computers, in case of a failure. They are named A–M and are maintained by a handful of different companies, groups, and colleges. A few of these are Verisign, University of Maryland, U.S. Army Research Lab, and ICANN.

TCP/IP

After the IP address has been obtained, the client's request can be sent to the server by using the protocols TCP and IP, often referred to collectively as **TCP/IP**. Even though these protocols are almost always paired together, they handle two separate steps in the process. On the client side, TCP is the next step. In this step, the request is broken down into smaller, more manageable pieces called **packets**. TCP also numbers these packets, so when they are put back together (on the server side), they will be in the correct order. When TCP finishes, the packets are handed off to IP. IP then creates and attaches addresses to each packet. This creates a way to keep track of all the packets as they travel across the physical Internet.

Fault Tolerant

Since the packets are numbered, it is easy for TCP to keep track of missing packets. If the server or host sees that packet number 25 is missing, it will request it again. Once the packet makes it to the destination, it is reassembled into the original file. This ensures that all packets eventually make it to the correct destination. The Internet is **fault tolerant** since if there is an error, the system will still work properly. Without this property, the whole system could fail if a single packet was misplaced.

Modems

Before any of this data can travel anywhere, it must first be converted (or modulated) from ones and zeros to the appropriate signal (light, electricity, or radio waves). A **modem** is the device that handles both the *mo*dulation, for outgoing signals, and the *dem*odulation, for incoming signals. It is common to see consumer products that serve as an all-in-one router and modem.

Routers

Once the DNS, TCP, and IP have done their work, the data is sent to a networking device used to direct Internet traffic called a **router**. In home networks, routers are usually plugged into (or part of) a modem. The newly made packets are sent to this router first. This personal router then sends the packets to the ISP's routers, and from here they are sent to many different routers along the "route" to the client. These packets are trying to find the fastest route possible, so if there is high traffic at one router, they will take a different path. Much like roadways in the US, if there is a major accident or traffic jam, the cars (packets) will take a different road. The TCP/IP's job of numbering and addressing the packets is important in case some packets don't make the trip. This is not uncommon. The client will simply ask for the missing packets by number instead of repeating the entire request. When the server receives these packets, it does the same process in reverse.

The server first collects the bits and turns them into packets then IP arranges them into order and TCP turns the packets back into a message. The request is then processed and sent back to the client in the same manner.

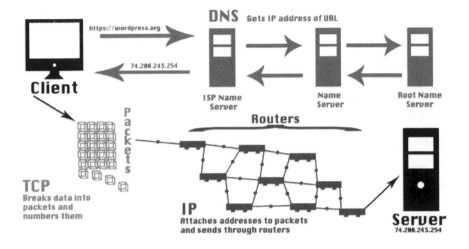

The Internet Infrastructure

The closest part of the Internet's physical infrastructure, as mentioned above, is the first router that data is sent to. This router is usually a local business or home router. The data then gets sent to the ISP's router. For Internet provided over a cell signal (4G, LTE, etc.), the router is stored at the cell tower's location. Once the data reaches the ISP's initial point of contact, the packets are then sent through several more routers that are connected to the previous router by one of three mediums: electricity, light, or radio waves.

Electricity

One way to send these packets from one router to the next is by using copper wires. These copper wires send pulses that get converted in to ones and zeros. Copper wire is found in most of the wires seen when connecting routers over a short distance and includes telephone wires (dial-up), DSL (another way to use telephone lines), Ethernet (cat5/6 cables), and cable Internet (coaxial). Category 5 and 6 cables are the predominant way electricity is used for networking today. Referred to as simply cat5 or cat6, these cables use twisted pairs (a method of twisting two wires together to reduce interference) to send signals through copper wires. There are a few downsides to using these cables. First, the signal can become degraded when sent over a long distance. Second, these wires are affected by electrical disturbances, such as lightning. Since there is less interference, cable is usually faster than wireless, but not nearly as fast as the speed of light.

Light

The fastest way to send packets, especially over long distances, is by using infrared light in the form of hair thin, transparent fibers called fiber optic cables (either single-mode or multimode). Not only is using fiber optic cables faster, but they can also use a higher bandwidth and are not disturbed by electromagnetic interference. Fiber optic cables can consist of a pair up to several hundred pairs of fibers that can transmit light pulses that get converted back into ones and zeros by modems.

The two main types of fiber optic cable and are single- and multimode cables. **Multimode cables** are thicker (about 62.5 microns) than single-mode (about 10 microns) and can send light at different wavelengths through the same fiber. These extra wavelengths result in higher bandwidth but cause distortion over long distances (more than a few miles). For longer distances, **single-mode cable** is used. These are thinner and carry just one wavelength or mode but can carry a signal across very long distances.

While fiber optics are becoming more prevalent in large cities, these cables are most common in large underwater systems that connect continents. An interactive map of the cables resting at the bottom of oceans and where they connect to land can be seen on TeleGeography's website (https://www.submarinecablemap.com/). Once the data reaches land, it travels from router to router until it arrives at the correct location. Since this data is traveling at the speed of light, it takes a fraction of a second to travel from Europe to the United States. Most of the cable's girth is used to protect the hair-thin fibers that send the data thousands of miles in a split second.

Radio

The final way to transfer data is by radio waves. Radio waves are the part of the electromagnetic (EM) spectrum from 3 Hz to 3000 GHz. Since these waves exist on the EM spectrum, they travel at the speed of light—in theory. However the Earth is not a vacuum, so some mediums (gas, water, air, glass) slow the signal down while other things (cement, wood, humans) absorb some of the signal.

Some frequencies on the electromagnetic spectrum are used for AM and FM radio, television, satellite radio, microwaves, GPS, other forms of communication, and of course many Internet related transmissions. These frequencies are usually assigned by a branch of each country's government, especially since some frequencies do not travel very far. Lower frequencies travel farther since there is less electromagnetic interference and they can pass through objects better. With so many towers available nowadays, high frequencies can be just as useful. US frequency allocations are public and are provided by the US Department of Commerce. Most television, cell phones GPS, Wi-Fi, Bluetooth, walkie-talkie, and cordless phone signals are found in the UHF (ultra-high frequency) range, which spans 300 MHz to 3 GHz. The allocations are always changing as old technology becomes obsolete and new technology becomes more in-demand. The most popular wireless protocols are 802.11a (2.4 GHz), 802.11g (5 GHz), 802.11n (2.4/5 GHz), and now 802.11ad (60 GHz). The speeds of these protocols range from 6 megabits/second (802.11a) all the way up to 6.7 gigabits/second (802.11ad).

Speed
When sending digital data, everything is broken down to ones and zeros—or bits. The number of bits that can be processed per second is called the **bit rate**. The broader term **bandwidth** refers to the amount

of resources available to transmit data and is usually measured in bit rate or frequency. **Latency** is sometimes defined as the amount of delay when sending digital data over a network but is more commonly understood as the round-trip time information take to get from the client to the server and back. Latency is measured in milliseconds and can be found by pinging an IP address or URL. Since this data is traveling at the speed of light, latency between North America and Europe is less than 50 milliseconds. In other words, fast.

Since its origins as a communication tool for researchers, the Internet has grown to encompass nearly every aspect of modern life. Built on protocols—sets of rules—that allow computers on many different networks to communicate with each other, the Internet can seem like an amorphous, non-material thing: a cloud. But all this information is being sent through a physical infrastructure made up of modems, routers, and servers, each sending signals to the other using electricity, light, and radio waves. While the Internet includes numerous protocols and is more than just the World Wide Web, for many, the Hypertext Transfer Protocol (HTTP)—the set of rules for transmitting websites—is synonymous with the Internet. In the following unit, we turn to the tools you need to create your own websites: HTML and CSS.

Important Vocabulary

- **ARPANET** – the Advanced Research Projects Agency Network, the first network to use TCP/IP

- **Bandwidth** – the amount of resources available to transmit data

- **Client** – any computer that requests a service

- **Cloud computing** – using a remote server to store files

- **DNS** – Domain Name System, one of the smaller networks that make up the Internet. It contains many servers that act like phone books

- **Domain Name** – a name given or linked to an IP address

- **Fault Tolerant** – a property of IP. If there is an error, it still works properly

- **FTP** – File Transfer Protocol, used for transferring files between a client and a server

- **HTML** – Hyper Text Markup Language, the standard markup language for creating web pages

- **HTTP** – Hyper Text Transfer Protocol, used for websites

- **HTTPS** – a secure version of HTTP that uses SSL/TLS

- **IMAP** – Internet Message Access Protocol, used for email

- **Internet** – a network of smaller networks connected using specific sets of rules that computers use to communicate with each other

- **IP** – Internet protocol, a set of rules for sending packets over the Internet

- **IP Address** – a unique identifier for every device on the Internet
- **IPv4** – the version of IP that uses 32-bit addresses
- **IPv6** – the version of IP that uses 128-bit addresses
- **ISP** – Internet Service Provider
- **Latency** – the amount of delay when sending digital data over the Internet or the round-trip time information takes to get from the client to the server and back
- **MAC (media access control) Address** – a unique, physical address that is stored in the computer's ROM
- **Modem** – a device that handles both the modulation and the demodulation of signals
- **Name Server** – a server that contains many IP addresses and their matching domain names
- **Network** – a group of computers that are connected so they can share resources using a data link
- **Packets** – small chunks of data used in TCP/IP
- **POP** – Post Office Protocol, used for email
- **Protocol** – a specific set of rules
- **Root Name Server** – one of thirteen servers that contain every IP address and its matching domain name
- **Router** – a networking device that routes Internet traffic to the destination
- **Server** – any computer that provides a service

- **Subdomain** – precedes the domain name, owned by the domain *https://subdomain.domain.com*

- **TCP** – Transmission Control Protocol, a set of rules for breaking down requests into smaller, more manageable, numbered packets

- **UDP** – User Datagram Protocol, like TCP and usually used for streaming media

- **URL** – Uniform Resource Locator, specifies where to find a file on a domain

- **VoIP** – Voice over Internet Protocol, used for telephony

- **Web (World Wide Web)** – the part of the Internet that uses HTTP and HTTPS

Suggested Reading

- "You Can't Say That on the Internet." *Blown to Bits*. Chapter 7. Pages 229-257

- "Bits in the Air." *Blown to Bits*. Chapter 8. Pages 259-294

- "The Internet as System and Spirit." *Blown to Bits*. Appendix. Pages 301-316

- "Search Engine Indexing." *Nine Algorithms that Changed the Future*. Chapter 2. Pages 13-22

- "PageRank." *Nine Algorithms that Changed the Future*. Chapter 3. Pages 23-31

Unit 6 – HTML, CSS, and Adobe Dreamweaver

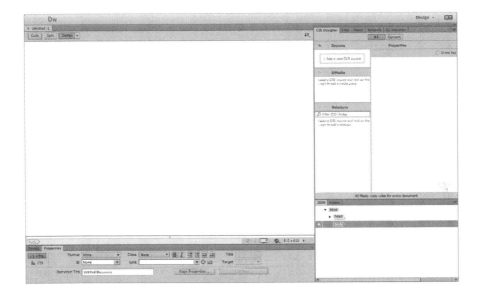

Primary learning outcomes met in this chapter: Creativity, The Internet. Programming

Introduction to Adobe Dreamweaver

Since Tim Berners-Lee first deployed HTTP in 1989, the World Wide Web has grown to a previously unimaginable scale, and websites have gained ever greater levels of complexity. In order to craft complex and aesthetically pleasing websites, a web development application—like Adobe Dreamweaver—is a useful tool. Originally created by Macromedia, Dreamweaver is now developed by Adobe Systems, which acquired Macromedia in 2005.

Dreamweaver is available for both Mac and Windows operating systems. Recent versions have incorporated support for web technologies such as CSS, JavaScript, and various server-side scripting languages and frameworks including ASP, ColdFusion, and PHP.

Creating a New Website

Nearly every webpage on the Internet contains more than one file. It might have multiple pages, pictures, style sheets, or other assets. As a website becomes more complex, the number of files needed to make it work also grows. To keep these files or assets organized, websites will be stored in folders with many subfolders containing many other files.

To create a new site, click *Site...* *New Site...* on the menu bar. When the following window comes up, give the site a name next to *"Site Name."* This name will be used inside Dreamweaver and will not be seen anywhere on the website itself. Next click the folder icon next to the text field labeled *"Local Site Folder."* This folder should be empty. It can be a previously existing folder, or it can be created when the folder icon is clicked.

Creating New Pages

Once a site has been defined, a folder with the site's files will show up in the Files panel on the bottom right hand side of the screen. For a new site, this folder will most likely be empty. To add a new page to the site, right click on the folder and select New File. If the new file is a web page, make sure the file extension is .html. You can also create new folders by right clicking. A new folder named assets should be created, which in turn will contain four new folders: images, css, fonts, js. These subfolders will contain any images, style sheets, unique fonts, and JavaScript files, respectively.

Views

At the top left of the file window, there are three buttons that let the user change the view of the website. These views are code, split, and design/live. Code shows behind-the-scenes stuff, such as the html and css code. Design/live shows what the page will look like in a web browser. Split allows the other two views to be open simultaneously.

Sometimes it is easier to change content on a webpage in the design view, but the live view is helpful to get a better idea of how the site will appear in a browser. Some CSS elements will not show up in the design view, nor will responsive webpages that change depending on the width of the page. Both design and live views have their own advantages.

Properties Panel

The properties panel is located at the bottom of the screen. Depending on what is selected on the page, different properties will be displayed. There are formatting options here for text, such as color and font. *Do not use these to change the look of text!* There are many useful things that show up in the properties panel, including links and page properties, but *not text formatting.* Text formatting will be done through CSS.

Adding Pictures and Links

To add a picture, simply save the image into the *images* folder and then drag the picture onto the page. Use the properties panel to change the size, ID, source, class, alt tag, and more. There are also tools to modify the image, crop it, and even open it in Photoshop.

Links are also found on the properties panel. Simply copy and paste any URL into the text field labeled "Link." If an existing webpage on the site is the desired link then drag the target symbol to the HTML file or image on the "Files" tab. Alternatively, click on the folder icon and select the file. If you wish to have the link open in a new window or tab, change the "Target" dropdown to the desired action.

Forms

The "Form" dropdown in the "Insert" tab is an easy way to access form elements, such as check boxes, text fields, radio buttons, checkboxes, buttons, and more—all of which will be used in the JavaScript chapter of this book.

CSS

Cascading Style Sheets (CSS) is a style sheet language used to describe the presentation—that is the look and formatting—of a document written in a markup language. The most common application is to style web pages written in HTML. CSS is designed primarily to enable the separation of document content (written in HTML or a similar markup language) from document presentation, including elements such as the colors, fonts, and layout. This separation can improve accessibility, provide more flexibility and control over presentation characteristics, enable multiple pages to share formatting, and reduce complexity and repetition in structural content, such as by allowing for table-less web design. CSS also allows the same markup page to be presented in different styles for different rendering methods, such as on screen or in print, on a specific device, or depending on screen width and resolution. While the author of a document typically links the document to a specific CSS style sheet, readers can use a different style sheet, perhaps one on their own computer, to override the one the author has specified.

CSS specifies a priority scheme to determine which style rules apply in case more than one rule applies to an element. In this so-called cascade, priorities or weights are calculated and assigned to rules, so the results are predictable.

Rules

There are three general types of CSS rules: tag, class, and ID. While in the "CSS Designer" tab, click the plus sign next to the "Selector" section. Dreamweaver will automatically try and guess what you are trying to add by looking at the currently selected element. To makes changes, simply delete the text and write the desired rule.

The first type of rule is the **tag rule** which will redefine what an HTML tag looks like, including **body, h1, h2, h3, a, div, img,** and many more. The word tag here refers to the HTML tags in the document. There are over 90 available, but only a handful of them will be used often. The names of all the tags on an element can be seen at the bottom of the design view in the tag inspector bar, above the properties palette. A few of the most common ones are **body**, the heading tags (**h1-h6**), the anchor tag for links (**a**), **div** tags, the paragraph tag (**p**), and the image tag for pictures (**img**). As websites become more complex, more tags will be used.

The **class rule** will be applied to any HTML tag belonging to a specific class. Their names always *begin with a period*. Once added to the CSS, these classes will show up in the "Class" dropdown found in the "Properties" panel. Class rules can be applied to any type and any number of HTML elements. They can even be added to small parts of elements like paragraphs or headings by automatically adding the <span> tags around the selection. Remember, the text formatting buttons should not be used, so class tags are the best way to bold, underline, or italicize things. Class tags can do countless other things, such as putting borders on tags, changing fonts or background colors, aligning elements, and adding padding or margins.

To add a rule to one specific element, **ID rules** are used. Since IDs are unique names for elements, each ID must be different. To add IDs to elements, find the "ID" text field in the "Properties" panel. To create the rule for the ID, name it *beginning with the pound/hash symbol (#)*. If the CSS rule for an ID is created before using an ID in the HTML then this ID will show up in the "ID" dropdown section in the "Properties" panel.

There are also pseudo class selector rules, which include link:, visited:, :hover, and :active. They are usually preceded by the *a* tag (e.g. - a: visited) but can be used on any tag (e.g. - h2: hover). The cascading nature of CSS means that the rules at the bottom of the list happen last, so for links these rules should be created in the above order. If *hover* were to be listed above *visited* in the CSS, then hover would only work if the link had not been visited yet.

Rules inside of rules can also be used, such as **div #container h1**. This rule would only be applied to an *h1* tag inside a *div* tag with the *ID* "container." If the same property needs to be added to multiple elements, they can be named and separated by commas: **#container, h1, h2, .highlight.**

Defining CSS Rules

So what kinds of things can these different CSS rules do?

There are five sections on the right-hand "CSS Designer" Property panel that will jump down to the corresponding section of the menu: Layout, Text, Border, Background, and More. Many of the menus are self-explanatory: *type* is the font for the specific rule; *background* is the background; and *border* is the border around the rule. There is also a "Show Set" checkbox in the top right corner of this panel. If this box is checked then only the styles being used will been shown. To see all styles, make sure this box is unchecked.

A commonly used property in this panel is "margin and padding." These modify the box, which is an invisible border around all tags and is very useful when sizing and laying out the webpage. The box can easily be seen if a border or background is added to the rule.

By default, a tag's width is 100% of the page, and its height is only as tall as needed to fit the material. These proportions can be changed using "width and height" under the "box" menu. *Float* determines what side of the page the tag is aligned to—left by default. *Padding* refers to the inside of the box and controls how close things are to the inside edge (think of a padded cell, which keeps the person inside away from the hard wall). *Margin* is the outside of the box and sets how close other tags can come to the edge.

@Media Queries

In addition to using CSS to change the look of the page, it can also be used to change the look of many other media queries. These queries include conditions that will check to see if the user is looking at a print preview, whether they are in landscape or portrait mode on a tablet or cell phone, and what their screen resolution is. There are many other conditions, including the most important one, max-width.

Max-width will check to see how wide the screen is and use the defined styles for this width. This is important when designing websites that respond to the device being used. A website should not look the same on a large desktop display and on a mobile phone. For example, little or no padding will be displayed on cell phones since real estate is scarce on such a small screen. Also, images may be different sizes on cell phone screens or even removed altogether.

To add these media queries, simply click the plus sign next to "@Media" in the "CSS Designer" panel. In this pop-up box, there will be at least one drop-down menu for any given condition. Multiple conditions can be added by clicking the plus sign that will show up when the cursor hovers over the current condition. This feature is useful when, for example, you need to define what a website looks like when displayed both in landscape mode *and* at a specific aspect ratio. Once the media query is added, add styles while the new media query is selected. The cascading property of CSS will make sure the new styles take effect since they are below the others on the style sheet. When defining different styles based on width, a common set of break points are devices larger than 1200 pixels (large desktops), between 992 pixels and 1199 pixels (regular desktops and tablets in landscape mode), between 768 pixels and 991 pixels (most tablets in portrait mode), and smaller than 767 pixels (most smart phones). When these are added to the media query, they can be seen in the live view (see above image) at the top of the page.

On a desktop, website content will move when the size of the window is changed. To avoid this, a container div tag (simply a div tag surrounding everything in the site with the ID: container) with a set width is used on the two largest screen sizes (e.g. width: 950px). Since tablet and smartphone screen sizes cannot be changed, it is appropriate to use percent of the screen when setting the width of a container div tag (e.g. width: 90%). It is also important to note that margins and padding will affect the percentage of a tag. This means that if a div tag is set to 100% and other elements around it have padding or margin, the width may be more than 100% of the page. To ensure that the page cannot scroll to the left or right, make sure that the total width of the elements does not add up to more than 100%.

CSS Designer   Files   Insert   Snippets   CC Libr
All
+   −   Sources : bootstrap.css (Read Onl...
ALL SOURCES
bootstrap.css (Read Only)
@Media
GLOBAL
print
(min-width : 768px)
(min-width : 768px)
(min-width : 768px)
(min-width : 992px)
(min-width : 1200px)
(min-width : 768px)
(min-width : 992px)
(min-width : 1200px)
screen and (max-width : 767px)
screen and (-webkit-min-device-pixel-ratio : 0)
(min-width : 768px)
(min-width : 768px)

Bootstrap

Bootstrap is the most popular HTML, CSS, and JS framework for developing responsive, mobile first projects on the web. First released in August 2011, it has since had more than twenty releases.

The entire framework—as well as all the documentation—can be found and downloaded at *getbootstrap.com*. The download contains everything needed to start a site, including CSS files, JavaScript files, and fonts. Luckily, Dreamweaver already stores all this information, which can be accessed by choosing the *Bootstrap* tab under "New Document" → *"HTML."* It is important to have already set-up the website (*site… new site* from earlier in this chapter), otherwise all the assets will be saved in whatever the most recent file's folder is. Uncheck the *'Include a pre-built layout"* checkbox to start fresh.

All the Bootstrap files and folders should now be visible in the *File* tab. This includes a css folder with a read-only bootstrap.css file, a fonts folder with various files, and a js folder with a couple JavaScript files. To get the index.html page into the root folder, simply click *file save* and rename the blank html page as index.html. It should be in the correct folder already. Since the CSS file is read-only, it cannot be modified. This is intentional. Since style sheets cascade, a new style sheet can be created below the read-only one. To do this, click the plus sign next to 'Sources" in the "CSS Designer" tab and select 'Create A New CSS File.*" Save this into the appropriately named "css" folder. Styles can be created or overwritten here. An appropriate name for this file could be "custom.css."

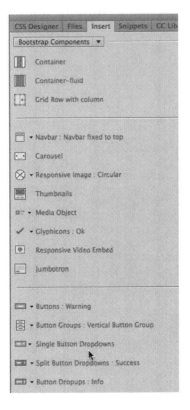

Once the Bootstrap files are set up, Bootstrap components can be added to the blank HTML page (remember to work in the "live" view to best see these components). A list of components can be found on the "Inset" tab's drop-down menu under "Bootstrap Components."

These components can be added by dragging them into the body in the live view, but they may not respond in the desired way. To drag a component into another component or tag (div, p, h1, etc.), drag and hover over the element until the inside edges glow blue. To put the component before or after the element, look for a green bar while hovering. Again, these might not act in the desired way or end up in the desired position.

To better place components, select the element above or below where it should go and click—don't drag—the component. A pop-up will appear giving options to place the new component before, after, nested, or—sometimes—wrapped around the selected element. Likewise, it may be easier to place components in the correct spot by dragging over the **</>** symbol and using the DOM representation of the page.

With the skills introduced in this chapter, you will be able to start creating your own websites that will adapt to whatever display they're viewed on, whether that is a giant desktop monitor or a tiny smartphone. The original vision of the World Wide Web imagined a decentralized space where anyone could have their own website, linked to other websites through hyperlinks. With the rise of Facebook, Instagram, Twitter, and other social media sites, much creative expression on the Internet has moved into these corporate controlled "walled gardens," isolated from the wilds of the Web. While these companies provide valuable and enjoyable services, in so doing, they collect an enormous amount of information. We turn to this information—known as big data—in the next unit.

Unit 7 – Big Data and Security

Primary learning outcomes met in this chapter: Algorithms, Global Impact

Big Data

Data is everywhere. People have always collected information for multiple purposes. Data used to be relatively simple. Early humans recorded where they could find food and tracked weather patterns. With advancing technologies, however, data has become easier to collect and subsequently used for many more purposes. In the last 50 years, tracking television viewing habits has led to the current state of TV and targeted advertising. With this data, companies and advertising agencies can better target the consumers who are interested in their products. These companies save millions of dollars by not wasting money on consumers who are unlikely to by their products while increasing sales by targeting their ads at the more-likely-to-buy consumers.

Big data often refers to sets of data that are larger than a consumer software application can handle. This could be data collected from hundreds of sources, including mobile phones, software, web browser logs, cameras, and wireless networks. A few key features of big data are the volume of the data, the rate at which it is collected, the variety of types, and the fact computers can "learn" from it. The volume is important since it is not a sample of data from different groups of people: It is all the data from all the people, so there is—in principle—less room for error. The rate at which data is collected is also important since, with the speed of processors and fiber optics, the data is in real-time. The variety of big data allows text, audio, video, and more all to be collected simultaneously and analyzed. This allows the data to be seen from different angles, making the results even more accurate. Finally, computers can see trends and patterns in this data that would take humans many lifetimes to sift through. Not only can computers see the trends, but they can also learn from them and use them when analyzing similar data in the future. Big data is very powerful and companies pay top dollar to obtain it.

In 2012 Facebook bought Instagram for $1 billion. That is billion—with a "B." Any programmer at Facebook easily could have designed an app that did the exact same thing as Instagram, probably with improvements. So why pay one-thousand million dollars for an app? At the time, Instagram had 30 million users, and it had a lot of data about those 30 million users. This data included how often they were on the app, how long they used the app per session, what profiles they looked at, what pictures they liked, all their search results, and more. The app itself was not worth $1 billion, but the large data set Instagram collected and their daily active users were worth that much to Facebook.

Big data is seen in many other industries, including government, education, media, healthcare, banking, real estate, retail, and more. The app Waze (acquired by Google for almost $1 billion) uses every user's data, even when the app is not open. When installed, the user gives permission to always use their location. If the user's geolocation is on a road then the app can record their speed. This information can be used to predict traffic and help reroute other users in real-time.

Security

With all this sensitive and valuable data being transferred every second, it is important to keep it secure. You probably would not yell your social security number or credit card number across a crowded room. Similarly, you should not send this data through insecure methods. There are several ways that malicious security **hackers** — "black hats" who exploit weaknesses on a computer or network—can steal or disrupt data. Some of these hackers just want to harm or break a network while others want to gather this data for other purposes, including identity theft or obtaining credit card numbers. Not all hackers seek to do harm. A hacker is any skilled user of technology who uses their prowess to solve problems. "White hat" security hackers explore the vulnerabilities on a computer or network—with the owner's consent—in order to help fix weaknesses and make data more secure.

One way hackers can perform these harmful tasks is by installing a **virus** on a computer or server. A virus is a program that infects other programs and usually spreads to other programs or computers by copying itself repeatedly. Most viruses spread due to user behavior.

Opening an email attachment from an unknown source or plugging an infected USB drive into a computer can cause a virus to be installed. Once installed, it is hard to remove a virus since it masks itself as other programs. Luckily, today's anti-virus software can catch most of these threats.

Another way hackers try to obtain this data is by **phishing** — using "bait" to trick the user into entering sensitive information like user names, passwords, or credit card numbers. Hackers create a fake site or email that looks identical to a trustworthy website and try to get the user to log in or update their info. Instead of logging in to the real site, though, the info is sent directly to the hackers, who can easily test your user name and password combination on hundreds of other sites in a matter of seconds. One way users can protect themselves is by always making sure the URL is the correct URL for the real site. Any site can add a subdomain to the beginning of their URL, so https://amazon.com and http://amazon.ft543ffj.com are completely different domains (the actual site is ft543ffj.com). Another way users can protect themselves is by making sure they never use the same password for more than one website.

Password strength is equally important. Many users think if they use a number and a symbol in their password then it will be hard to crack. This is not the case. The main way to increase the strength of a password is by making it longer. Hackers compile a list of passwords they find every time data is data stolen. If a user's password is on that list, it would take no time at all to break into their accounts. The hackers can even test all these passwords to see if there is an at sign (@) in place of an A or a dollar sign ($) in place of an S, so these common substitutions do not increase password strength. Since length is the main indicator of a strong password, something like "*Bhdiu3fbEieef$nei3rf*" would be great, but it is doubtful anyone would — or could — memorize a password like that for every site they visit. Password management sites — like *1Password.com*, *LastPass*, and *KeePass* — can be used to generate and store these random passwords. Another technique is to combine four or more random words into one long word. If one of the words is obscure, that's even better, so a great password that is easier to remember than random characters could be "paperelephantchartreusecoconut." This is longer than the previous example but much easier to remember. It's a good practice to use a password like this one to log in to a password management site and to have this site store different, long, and random sets of characters for all other sites. This way, you only need to memorize one password. It should go without saying that you should keep this password secret — and don't use the example from this book!

Another method hackers use to cause havoc for a website is to use a **distributed denial-of-service attack (DDoS)**. In this method, hackers flood a site with fake requests, making the site's resources unavailable for legitimate users. This method does not steal any information or try to install any viruses, it simply hurts the site's business. There are many possible motives for a DDoS attack including spite, revenge, and blackmail. There are many defenses against DDoS attacks, including blocking certain IP addresses and firewalls.

Cryptography

The most basic form of cryptography — methods for sending data securely in the presence of an adversary — is **encryption**, which is simply taking text and converting it so that it is illegible. The reverse process — converting the illegible text back into legible text — is known as **decryption**. To be able to encrypt and decrypt data, a list of instructions is needed. A **cipher** is a pair of **algorithms** — the list of instructions — that give details on how to encrypt and decrypt the data. There is also a shared secret — or **key** — that is needed to make the encryption harder to crack.

Types of Ciphers

One famous cipher is the **Caesar cipher** or Caesar shift where each letter is shifted the same amount. So if the shift (or key) was set to 1, then "A" would become "B"; "R" would become "S"; "X" would become "Y"; and "Z"" would loop around to the beginning of the alphabet and become "A." If the shift was 10, it would move each letter 10 places ahead and "A" would become "K." To decrypt the message, simply shift the key backwards.

Example:

> **Key:** 14
>
> **Plain text:** Computer Science is fun
>
> **Encrypted text:** Qcadihsf Gqwsbqs wg tib

This is a very simple cipher to use, but patterns of letters make it simple to crack or decipher. With computers, it would be solved in a split second.

Another example of simple encryption is the **random substitution cipher**. In this cipher, a letter is mapped or swapped with another letter in the alphabet, so "A" could be mapped to "F"; "B" could be mapped to "Z"; "C" could be mapped to "A" and so on until all 26 letters were mapped to another letter.

Example:

ABCDEFGHIJKLMNOPQRSTUVWXYZ

> **Key:** SGPFNEYQUJKRCDVMIZAXHWOLBT
>
> **Plain text:** Computer Science is fun
>
> **Encrypted text:** Pvcmhxnz ua ehd

This seems much harder to crack than the Caesar cipher, but it also has patterns, which makes it easy to break. This can be done quickly by a computer, but it can also be done by hand by looking at reoccurring sets of letters and letter frequency. The letter "E" is the most common letter in the English language, so whatever letter shows up most in the encrypted text is probably mapped to "E." If the same three letters appear multiple times, this could be the word "the," solving three letters at once.

A more difficult cipher to crack is the **Vigenère cipher**, which has similarities to the Caesar cipher and dates to the 1460s. As with the Caesar cipher, the Vigenère cipher uses a key to set the amount of letters the message will shift, but in the Vigenère cipher, the key is much longer and not the same for every letter. If the key was a phrase like "applesaretasty" then the first 14 characters would shift according to what letter was in the key at that place. The first letter would shift by "A" or 1, the second and third by "P" or 16, and so on. The fifteenth letter would start back at the beginning of the key. This process would then repeat itself until the whole text is encrypted.

Even though this cipher is difficult to crack, patterns and letter frequencies can still be used to find the key. The only way to make it unbreakable would be to have a key that was longer than the text itself, removing any patterns that arise (one-time pads use this method).

Example (assuming "_" is the 27th letter):

Key: APPLESARETASTY

Plain text: COMPUTER_SCIENCE_IS_FUN

Encrypted text: CCA_YKEHDKC_XKCTOTWRFKR

A famous example of breaking ciphers and decrypting messages can be seen in the film *The Imitation Game*, which tells the true story of Alan Turing, an English mathematician—he would be called a computer scientist today—who helped crack the German **Enigma machine** during World War II, allowing the Allies to read encrypted German messages and shortening the war by several years. A YouTube search will turn up videos that show exactly how the machine worked and how it was eventually cracked.

Public Key Encryption

When talking about encryption, it is common to refer to two people communicating with each other while another tries to listen in. Traditionally, these two people are named **Alice** and **Bob** while the eavesdropper is called **Eve** (get it?). To use any of the previously discussed cipher examples, a shared key is needed that no one else knows. This type of key is called a **private key**. If Alice and Bob both know the private key and Eve does not then encryption and decryption are simple. Eve will not be able to read the message between Alice and Bob, even if she intercepts it. Without the private key, the message looks like jumbled characters. Since Alice and Bob each use the same key both to encrypt and decrypt the message, it is known as

symmetric key encryption. This method works well to send secret messages, but the problem is obtaining the private key. What if Alice is in New York and Bob is in Tokyo? If they try to send the key to each other then Eve can intercept it and decrypt any future messages.

Public key encryption is a system that allows Alice and Bob to publicly publish a key that everyone, including Eve, can see. One way to think about public keys is by considering padlocks. Encrypting a message using Bob's public key is like putting a padlock on the message that only Bob has the key to, so if Alice wants to send an encrypted message to Bob, she encrypts it using Bob's public key. Only Bob has the information needed to unlock the "padlock" and read the message. Since the encryption key is different than the decryption key, public key encryption is also known as **asymmetric key encryption**.

How Public Key Encryption Works

Public key encryption creates a problem that is computationally hard, like in the traveling Salesman dilemma in unit four. A computer could crack the cipher, but it would take several super computers hundreds or even thousands of years (Unless and until quantum computers become widely available. These machines could theoretically make cracking current encryption algorithms trivially easy). Even though public key is tough to break, it is very simple to use. A problem that is easy in one direction and difficult in the other is known as a **one-way function**. Another one-way function, which is used in public keys as well, is clock or **modular arithmetic**. Imagine that an analog clock was set to 12:00 then someone moved the hour hand to 3:00. It might appear that the hour hand was only moved ahead 3 hours, but it could have been moved ahead a full rotation plus 3 hours which is 15 hours or 2 full rotations plus 3 hours which is 27 hours. It could have been moved ahead an infinite number of rotation plus 3 hours. It is impossible to know. The only person who has this information is the person that moved the clock ahead. This problem is easy for the person moving the clock hand but impossible for anyone who does not know how many rotations were made. In a very broad way, this is how public key encryption works.

Types of Public Key Encryption

Two of the most commonly used public key encryption algorithms are **Diffie-Hellman** (named after Whitefield Diffie and Martin Hellman) and **RSA** (named after Ron Rivest, Adi Shamir, and Leonard Adleman). Diffie-Hellman was one of the first public key encryption protocols and dates to the mid-1970s. Diffie-Hellman is considered a key exchange algorithm, a way to swap the private keys needed for other encryption algorithms.

RSA followed Diffie-Hellman. In addition to asymmetric encryption, it also allows for **digital signature**. The digital signature is an electronic signature that, by using a public key, can be verified to be authentic. Both these algorithms are integral in security today.

Public Key Security Certificates

Another application of public key encryption can be seen when browsing the web. It is important to trust the website being visited and also to have a secure connection, so Eve cannot see—or alter—what is being communicated between the user and the site. This happens every time **https://** is used. The "s" stands for secure and indicates that the Diffie-Hellman key exchange, RSA, or other methods are being used to secure the connection through a **digital handshake**. This process is called **Transport Layer Security (TLS)**. Its predecessor was **Secure Sockets Layer (SSL)**. TLS is the newer protocol, but this process is still referred to as SSL, even though TLS is used. Public key is used in SSL by authenticating a **Digital Certificate**, a trusted third-party file that verifies that the site is controlled by the legitimate owner. When possible, always use SSL (https) to visit websites. *HTTPS Everywhere* is a free and open source browser plug-in released by the Electronic Frontier Foundation and the Tor Project that forces https over http whenever possible.

Some of the largest and most profitable enterprises to ever exist in human history are built on the foundation of big data. In order to keep all this information secure, cryptography and other security practices are indispensable. As this book goes to press, data security and privacy are front-page news and the subject of heated congressional hearings. Given the power and profits built on the control of this information, the debate over who owns data, how it should be protected, and what it can be used for is unlikely to be resolved anytime soon. A basic understanding of the underlying technology is essential not just for computer users but for citizens. Similarly, code drives the modern economy, and the individuals, organizations, and countries that control critical algorithms have enormous power in the world today. Familiarity with the basics of programming—the topic of the following unit—will provide you with important skills for navigating the modern economy.

Important Vocabulary

- **Big Data** – sets of data that are larger than a consumer software application can handle
- **Hacker** – anyone who uses their technological skills to solve problems. A malicious security hacker exploits weaknesses on a computer or network and can steal or disrupt data
- **Virus** – a program that infects other programs and usually spreads to other programs or computers by copying itself repeatedly
- **Phishing** – using "bait" to trick a user into handing over sensitive information like user names, passwords, or credit card numbers
- **DDoS** – distributed denial-of-service attack, hackers flood a site with fake request making all the site's resources unavailable for legitimate users
- **Encryption** – taking text and converting it so it is illegible
- **Decryption** – the reverse process of encryption

- **Cipher** – a pair of algorithms that give details on how to encrypt and decrypt the data

- **Caesar Cipher** – a shift cipher where each letter is shifted the same amount

- **Digital signature** – an electronic signature that, by using public key, can be verified authentic

- **Digital Certificate** – a trusted third-party file that verifies a site as legitimate

- **Asymmetric key encryption** – a different key is used to encrypt and decrypt a message

- **Key** – in cryptography, a shared secret to make encryption harder to crack

- **Modular arithmetic** – using the remainder when dividing, also known as clock arithmetic

- **One-way Function** – a problem that is easy in one direction and difficult in the other

- **Private Key** – a shared secret needed to decrypt a message

- **Public Key** – a system that allows a key to be publicly published

- **SSL** – Secure Sockets Layer, issues digital certificates for websites

- **Substitution Cipher** – a cipher where a letter is mapped or swapped with another letter in the alphabet

- **Symmetric Key Encryption** – the same key is used both to encrypt and decrypt a message

- **TLS** – Transport Layer Security, issues digital certificates for websites

Suggested Reading

- "Secret Bits." *Blown to Bits*. Chapter 5. Pages 161-193
- "Public Key Cryptography." *Nine Algorithms that Changed the Future*. Chapter 4. Pages 32-46
- "Digital Signatures." *Nine Algorithms that Changed the Future*. Chapter 9. Pages 109-125

Unit 8 – Programming: JavaScript

Primary learning outcomes met in this chapter: Programming, Abstraction, Algorithms, Creativity

History and Usage

There are numerous programming languages in which software can be written. **Low-level languages** (binary, assembly, machine language, etc.) are considered "close to the metal" (that is the hardware) and have little or no abstraction. While these languages interface directly with the computer, which makes them run quickly, it is difficult for human beings to read or write them. **High-level languages** (C, Java, Python, etc.) are easier for humans to read, which makes them easier to debug. High-level languages also rely on abstraction and other already existing libraries. A compiler or interpreter turns a high-level language into a low-level language before it gets sent to the hardware.

Since JavaScript cannot stand alone—it needs a web browser to run—many consider it a scripting language and not a programming language, but JavaScript should still be considered a high-level language. First introduced in December 1995, JavaScript was originally developed by Brendan Eich of Netscape Communications Corporation. Along with HTML and CSS, JavaScript is one of the foundational technologies of the modern Web. JavaScript is a scripting language with a syntax loosely based on C. Like C, it has reserved keywords and no input or output constructs of its own. Where C relies on standard I/O libraries, a JavaScript engine relies on the host environment into which it is embedded, in our case a web browser.

Debugging

Depending on the development environment, debugging can prove to be quite difficult. Since errors in JavaScript only appear in run-time (i.e., there is no way to check for errors without executing the code) and since JavaScript is interpreted by the web browser as the page is viewed, it may be difficult to track down an error's cause. Today's web browsers, however, come with reasonably good debuggers. With the arrival of integrated toolbars and plug-ins, an increasing amount of support for JavaScript debugging has become readily available.

For inexperienced programmers, scripting languages are especially susceptible to bugs. Because JavaScript is interpreted, loosely-typed, and has varying environments (host applications), implementations, and versions, the programmer should take exceptional care to make sure the code executes as expected.

Development Process

In computer programming, the process of creating and developing software should be both iterative and incremental. It should be **incremental** in that it is done in small chunks and **iterative** in that it continuously repeats these steps. The main steps in this process are **design – implement – test**. The **design phase** consists of brainstorming and prototyping and is the most creative step in the process. The **implement phase** is putting the design into code. Since the design is already set, this phase should be the least creative. The **test phase** is checking to see if the code runs properly and finding errors or debugging the program. Since this process is iterative, the design phase is repeated after the test phase, and the program is constantly updated and improved. This process takes place every time a new version of software is released.

JavaScript

To insert JavaScript into HTML, you must use the <SCRIPT> tag. To close this tag when the JavaScript is complete, use the </SCRIPT> tag. JavaScript should be placed somewhere within the body of the HTML code, depending upon when the programmer wants to display their JavaScript program.

As with HTML, the computer does not read white space in JavaScript. Most commands in JavaScript, therefore, need to end in a semicolon to tell the computer when one command ends and another begins. JavaScript also uses programming's three basic logic structures: sequence, selection, and iteration. **Sequence** is the structure that runs one line after another, in order, without skipping or repeating code. So, after line 1 comes line 2 and after line 1001 comes line 1002. **Selection** uses *if statements* to select certain values, and **iteration** means to repeat a process. In programming this is accomplished by using loops. We will discuss selection and iteration in more detail below.

Comments are used to let the programmer—and anyone who looks at their code—know exactly what is going on. The programmer can use comments to define variables more clearly and to specify what they are trying to accomplish in certain areas of the program. Comments are especially helpful when going back to older projects after not looking at them for an extended period or when collaborating with others.

Using Variables

Variables are a way to store information. They can store many kinds of data, including text and numbers. Before they can be used, variables must first be defined. JavaScript uses the keyword **var** to set up a new variable. The word following **var** is the name of the new variable. The programmer may name this variable anything they would like. The name they choose should be relevant to what is being stored. For example: if the programmer is storing a string of text that says "Hello, how are you doing today?" then the variable might be called *greeting*. If the variable is storing someone's last name it might be called *lastName*. Notice that *lastName* is one word: Variables cannot have spaces nor can they start with anything except a letter. Also notice that the letter l in *lastName* is lower case while the N is upper case. This is called "camel casing" because the first letter is lower case and every new word is upper case, somewhat resembling a camel's humps. This is one way to avoid spaces. Using underscores is another way: *last_name*.

```
var greeting;
```

This line of code creates a variable named "greeting" that has nothing stored to it yet.

Strings

One thing a variable can store is a string, which is another way of saying text. A string may contain any character on the keyboard (even the space bar counts as a character). A string can be identified because it is surrounded by quotation marks. To create a string, the programmer must use quotation marks. "Hello, how are you?" is an example of such a string. Any input that is received from a prompt is in string form, even numbers.

```
greeting = "Hello, how are you?";
```

This line of code assigns the string "Hello, how are you?" to the variable "greeting."

Both creating the variable and assigning the variable can be combined into one step:

```
var greeting = "Hello, how are you?";
```

Numbers

A number differs from a string in that a string cannot be multiplied, rounded, or have any other mathematical operation applied to it. Another important difference is that, unlike strings, numbers do not have quotation marks around them.

```
var myAge = 17;
```

This command creates a variable named *myAge* and assigns it the value 17.

Alerts

The programmer can send a message to the user before they access the webpage. In JavaScript, this is called an *alert*. An alert pops up in a dialog box on the webpage. To make this happen, use the alert command:

```
alert("This is an alert!");
```

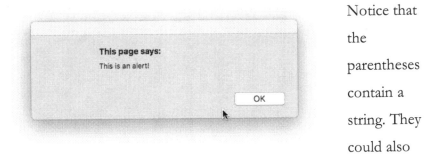

Notice that the parentheses contain a string. They could also

contain a number or a variable. Whatever is written in the parentheses will be displayed in the alert. The command must end in a semicolon to let the program know it is finished.

A variable can also be placed inside the parentheses. Remember that there are no quotation marks around a variable!

```
alert(greeting);
```

Prompts

Prompts are like alerts in that they pop up in a dialog box. The difference between prompts and alerts is that prompts ask the user for input. Since input is coming into the program, it needs to be stored somewhere. Recall that variables are used to store information and that all inputs are stored as strings. The **prompt("Enter input: ", "Default Text");** returns whatever the user enters into the prompt. To store this input, let's assign a variable to this prompt:

```
var userInput = prompt("Enter your input", "type
here");
```

This command stores the user's input with the variable *userInput*.

Concatenation

To combine two stings together, *concatenation* must be used. Concatenation is the combination of two strings. To concatenate two strings in JavaScript, use the "+" sign. This operator can be used as many times as needed in the program:

```
alert("Hello " + username +
        "how are you?");
```

Converting Strings into Numbers

Remember that any input to the program is stored as a string, so whenever a user inputs something into a prompt, it is stored as a string. This is a problem if a number is entered into the prompt. For example, if 17 is entered into the prompt, it will be stored as "17", a string. In order to apply math to a string, it must first be converted into a number. The command to do this is *parseInt( );* and *parseFloat( );* for integers and decimals (i.e. floating-point numbers) respectively. Again, this command returns a number, which must be stored somewhere. The programmer probably does not need to keep the string "17" stored, so whatever variable was used to store it can be written over:

```
var userAge = prompt("What is your age?", "Enter age
here");
userAge = parseInt(userAge);
```

The first line prompts the user to enter their age, which takes the form of a string. This string, which needs to be converted to a number, is inside the parentheses on the second line. The *userAge* on the left side of the second line is the new number.

Basic Math Operations

Now that there are numbers stored, mathematics can be applied to them. First, set up a new variable to store the solution then assign the equation to this variable. Addition (+), subtraction (-), multiplication (*), and division (/) can all be used here.

```
var dogAge = userAge * 7;
```

This line creates a new variable called *dogAge* and sets it to the user's age multiplied by 7.

Selection

Sometimes it is not necessary to run an entire script on a webpage. There are times when certain conditions need to be met to run a block of code. For example, if the user inputs their age, there could be a different alert for kids, teenagers, and adults.

If the user inputs an age below 13, they get one message. People between 14 and 17 get another message, and everyone 18 and older gets another. This allows the computer to decide between multiple cases, called **selection** in computer programming. Selection, along with sequence and iteration are the three logic structures in programming.

If Statements

The way to provide separate selections depending on the user's age can be accomplished by using **if statements**. An *if statement* begins with the word "if" (notice the lower-case "i"). The condition that needs to be met follows inside the parentheses. Conditions use the following symbols:

<	Less than
>	Greater than
<=	Less than or equal to
>=	Greater than or equal to
==	Equal to
!=	Not equal to

After the parentheses are closed around the conditional statement, braces { } are opened. *Notice: There is no semi-colon after the parentheses are closed!* If the conditional statement is true then anything that comes between these braces will be executed. If the conditional statement is not true, the code in the braces will be ignored.

A snippet of the code for the age program might look something like this:

```
if ( age <= 12 )
{
        alert("Enjoy your youth while it lasts!");
}
```

Else If Statements

If another *if statement* follows the first (usually conditions with the same variable), an **else if** can be used—this operator will connect the statements together. If the first *if statement* is true then the *else if statement* will be ignored. The order of the statements matters. These statements are exactly like *if statements* except for the word *else* before them.

This example might follow the snippet above:

```
else if ( age <= 17 )
{
        alert("Not too long before you can vote!");
}
```

Since the *if statement* above covers the ages 12 and below, this statement will only cover the ages from 13 to 17. Why you ask?

Well, if the age is 12 or below, the first *if statement* will be true, so the program will never get to the *else if statement*. There can be unlimited *else if statements* in the code.

Else Statements

The **else statement** can be used for any condition that is not met using the *if* or *else if statements*. The *else statement* works a little differently than the others because it does not need a conditional statement: It will only happen if the other statements are not true. In the age example, the *else statement* could look like this:

```
else
{
        alert("You are so old now!");
}
```

There can only be one *else statement* connected to each *if statement*, but the *else statement* is not necessary, nor is the *else if. But there can never be an* else if *or* else statement *without an* if statement!

Switch Statements

The **switch statement** is like the *if statement*, but rather than responding to conditions, the *switch statement* runs a segment of code for different cases. For example, the user might be asked to pick a number from a menu. The *switch statement* lets the programmer run different code depending on the user's input. The same thing could be accomplished with *if statements*, but it is much simpler with the *switch*.

The *switch* starts with the command:

```
switch(someVariable)
{
```

Notice: The block is opened with the open brace { (not a parenthesis)

someVariable is usually the variable that the user inputs. This variable can be anything from a single letter or number to a word or phrase. After the opening brace, the variable is compared to the available options and the appropriate code is run. In the *switch*, each option the programmer includes to be tested is called a *case*. To set up a case, simply write *case* followed by the desired input. If this desired input is a word or letter then it must be in quotation marks—unless you are using an existing variable. Numbers do not need quotation marks. A colon follows, which tells the computer that the code to run starts here. There can be as much or as little code as is needed. To tell the computer that the code is ending, the line **break;** is used. Without **break;**, the computer will not know the next case is beginning. Here are a few examples:

Example 1:

```
case 1:
        alert("You have picked choice number 1!");
        alert("You can have as much code as needed
        here...");
break;
```

```
case "yes":
        alert("You enter yes.");
        //all the code needed
        //even more code if necessary
   break;
   }
//when all cases are complete, make sure to close
the
//switch statement with a close brace
```

If there is something that the programmer wants to happen if none of the cases are met then the *default* case should be used. Instead of the word *case* followed by a case, simply write the word *default* followed by a semicolon. Remember JavaScript is case sensitive.

```
default:
        alert("None of the cases were met!");
```

Notice that the default case is not followed by the line **break;**. Since this case must be the last one, it does not need to tell the computer that a new case is about to begin.

Iteration

Iteration means to repeat a process. In programming, it is accomplished by using loops. A **loop** is a block of code that the programmer wants to run more than once. The number of times a loop is run could be different in each situation. A loop might need to be run an exact number of times (e.g. ten, one-hundred, etc.), or a loop might need to be run until a certain condition is met (e.g. until a counter reaches a number or until the user picks the correct answer to a question). Two kinds of loops are *for loops* and *while loops*.

For Loops

For loops are the loops that are used to run a loop an exact number of times. *For loops* have three parts: The user must first initialize a counter variable. They must set a condition for the loop to keep executing, and they must set the increment by which the counter changes. The first part initializes a counter variable. The most common name for this variable is i. The next part is a condition that tells the loop how long to run: This condition would include the variable that was just initialized. It might look like this: $i < 10$. This means if i is less than ten, the loop will continue to execute. The final part of this loop is the increment, which tells how much to increase or decrease the counter variable. If the programmer wants to increase the loop by 5 every time it executes, then they would type: $i = i + 5$;. To decrease by 20 every time, the programmer would use: $i = i - 20$; and so on. Since increasing and decreasing the counter by 1 is so common, there is a shorthand way to write it: $i++$ and $i--$. These three steps are contained in one set of parentheses, and each of the steps is separated by semicolons.

The block of code that is to be run in every loop is contained in braces. Together, the entire loop looks like this:

```
for( var i = 1; i < 10; i++ )
{
        Code to be run over and over goes here...
}
```

While Loops

A **while loop** is simpler than a *for loop*. *While loops* only have one part to them: the condition. For this reason, the programmer must set up a variable and make sure the condition is eventually met. An example of a *while loop* is prompting the user for a password. If the user guesses the incorrect password, the loop will continue to run, not letting user continue with the rest of the code.

```
var myPassword = "12345";
var userGuess = " ";
while( userGuess != myPassword)
{
        userGuess = prompt("Enter the
                password");
}
```

This code sets up two variables, one for the actual password and one for the user's guess. Notice that the user's guess is just set up as an empty string. The user has not guessed anything yet. The *while loop* has a condition that says, if the user's guess and the password are not equal, the loop will continue. Inside the loop is simply a prompt that asks the user to enter a password, so the program well continue to present the prompt to the user unless and until they enter the correct password.

Getting Stuck in Loops

The most common error with loops is using a condition that is always true. One case of this is if the programmer sets up a *for loop* that starts at one, whose condition is $i < 10$, and decreases i by one every time. If i loses one every time then the condition of $i < 10$ will always be true. Therefore the loop will never end. If the computer gets stuck in a loop, two things might happen: (1) there might be an alert that never goes away, causing the user to exit the program, or (2) the computer tries repeatedly to carry out something that will never happen and tells the user that the program is not responding. Make sure the loops are not endless before executing a program!

Multiple Conditions

Inside things with conditions, like *if statements* and loops, the programmer might want to have a case where more than one condition needs to be met or at least one condition of many is met. Here the **&& (AND)** and **|| (OR)** symbols can be used. The **&** symbol is found above the 7 key (hold down the shift key) and the **|** symbol is found above the **** key (which is found between the backspace and enter keys). In a situation where a variable called *age* needs to be between 18 and 25 then the code could look like this:

```
if ( age >= 18 && age <= 25)
```

If the situation called for the age to be either younger than 18 or at least 55, this code would be used:

```
if (age < 18 || age >= 55)
```

Many of these connectors can be used in a single conditional statement, as in the following code:

```
while ( age == 18 && weight < 400 && height > 42
        && hair == "blonde" && eyes == "blue")
```

Objects and Methods

JavaScript is an object-based programming language, which means that certain items in the language are stored as objects and that each of these objects has specific characteristics. Five important objects used in JavaScript are the **Math** object, the **document** object, the **string** object, the **Date** object, and the **array** object. Each of these objects has two features: *properties* and *methods*.

There are two different kinds of objects: objects that need to be set up by creating a new variable and those that can be used by simply saying the name of the object. The *new* keyword is used to create a new object to store in a variable, and this keyword needs to be used in the **date** and **array** objects. These objects will be discussed later in detail. The **string** object needs to be saved as a variable too, but the *new* keyword is not necessary. No variable needs to be set up for the **Math** and the **document** objects. Simply say *Math* or *document* when using these objects. Notice that *Math* is capitalized and *document* is all lowercase, JavaScript is CASE SENSITIVE.

Properties hold information about the object. In the *string* and the *array* objects, one property is *length*, which holds the length of the string or array. In the *Math* object *PI* is a property that holds the value of Π (approximately 3.14159). In the *document* object, some properties are *bgColor, fgColor,* and *title.* The *document* object deals with the webpage itself, so *bgColor* holds the background color, *fgColor* holds the foreground color, and the *title* is the title of the page. There are many other properties that can be found using a simple web search.

Methods are things the object can do. In the *Math* object, there are many methods, such as *sin, cos, tan, round, random, abs,* and *floor.* These methods *do* something to a number. They don't just hold information like properties do. In the string object, methods include *toUpperCase* and *toLowerCase.* These take a string and *do* something to them. They make them either into all uppercase or all lowercase letters. In the document object, there are the *open, write,* and *close* methods. Here the *open* method *does* something by opening the HTML file so the file can be written to using the *write* method. After the programmer is done writing to the HTML document, it needs to be closed using the *close* method.

In the date object, the important methods are *getDay, getDate, getMonth, getHours, getMinutes,* and *getSeconds.* These methods retrieve information, in the form of a number, about the specified part of the date.

The array object, has many methods as well. Some of the common array methods include *join, sort, concat,* and *reverse.* These methods will be addressed deeper into this chapter.

String Methods

Like numbers, strings may be manipulated in JavaScript. One common way to manipulate a string is to change it to all upper-case letters. To do this, we must call a method. Methods will be discussed in more detail later. To use this method, there must first be a string variable, which is just a variable with a string stored in it. *stringVar* will be the variable in this example. The period (.) is the way to call, or carry out, a method. Here the programmer would write the string variable, then a period, then the method. The output could be saved as another variable, or it could be placed directly into an alert. The method that is used to change strings to all CAPITAL LETTERS is **toUpperCase( )**.

Notice that this method does not have anything between the parentheses:

```
var stringVar = "this is my string";
alert(stringVar.toUpperCase( ));
```

Similarly, there is a way to return the length of a string. **.length** is the method that returns the number of characters in a string. Recall that a character is anything inside the string, including numbers, letters, symbols, and even spaces. This method can be called the same way as **toUpperCase( ),** and the result can also be stored as a variable or placed directly into an alert. Here is an example that finds the length of a greeting:

```
var greeting = "hello, how are you?";
alert(greeting.length);
```

Here is a project that combines all the concepts learned thus far:

```
<script>
var greeting = "Hello";
var firstName = prompt("What is your first
name?");
var lastName = prompt("What is your last name?");
var nameLength = firstName.length +
lastName.length;
alert(greeting + " " + firstName.toUpperCase( ) +
" " + lastName.toUpperCase( ));
alert("By the way, you have " + nameLength +
     " letters in your name");
</script>
```

This page says:
What is your first name?

Bob

Cancel   OK

This page says:
Hello BOB SMITH

☐ Prevent this page from creating additional dialogs.

OK

This page says:
By the way, you have 8 letters in your name

☐ Prevent this page from creating additional dialogs.

OK

Math Methods

To use one of the Math methods—or any method—the object must be called upon first. If the programmer wants to use the *round* method, first they would have to say *Math* (the object) then use a period to separate the object and the method. Together it looks like this:

```
Math.round(3.1415);
```

Here is a list of a few Math methods. More can be found in the appendix:

round(numVar);	Rounds to the nearest integer
ceil(numVar);	Rounds up to the nearest integer
floor(numVar);	Rounds down to the nearest integer
abs(numVar);	Returns the absolute value
sqrt(numVar);	Finds the square root of the number
pow(numVar, numVar);	Raises the 1st # to the 2nd #'s power
min(numVar, numVar, ...);	Returns the lowest of the numbers
max(numVar, numVar, ...);	Returns the highest of the numbers
random( );	Returns a random number between 0 and 1

Notice that the *random* method returns a number between 0 and 1. On its own, the usefulness of this method is extremely limited. A programmer is more likely to desire a random integer between, say, 1 and 10. To get this result, some math needs to be performed on the new number. First, multiply the random number by 10. Now it is a random number between 0 and 10—still not an integer. Next take the floor of the number—this makes the number an integer from 0 – 9. Finally, add 1 to the number to make it an integer between 1 and 10. These steps can be combined into one:

```
Math.floor( Math.random( )*10 ) + 1;
```

Note that the order of operations does matter here. To change how many random numbers there can be, simply change the factor by which .random( ) is being multiplied. To change the first number, add the new starting number where the 1 is.

Date Object

The Date object is a little different than the Math object in that it cannot be used simply by saying the name of the object. Like the string object, this object should be stored in a variable. In the string object, the assignment operator was all that needed to be used. In the Date object, this is not the case. To assign a new instance of an object to a variable, use the keyword *new*. When setting up a new instance of an object, the *new* keyword precedes the name of the object, which is followed by a set of parentheses, usually empty. A line that causes all the Date object's information to be stored in a variable called *d* would look like this:

```
var d = new Date( );
```

Now the programmer can use the methods associated with the Date object by placing the dot operator (a period) between the variable and the method:

```
var month = d.getMonth( )
```

This line will store the number of the month in a variable called *month*. This number will take the somewhat awkward form of a number from 0 – 11, January being 0 and December being 11. A simple switch statement can fix this to display the correct month number or name. Similar steps also need to be taken for the day of the week and hour of the day.

An example of the code to make the date print out properly is on the following pages.

The Date Object - Displaying Date and Time

```
<script>
var date = new Date();
var dom = date.getDate();
var dow = date.getDay();
var month = date.getMonth();
var year = date.getFullYear();    Create variable
at
var mins = date.getMinutes();              the top of
code
var hour = date.getHours();
var amPm = "a.m.";

switch(dow)
{
     case 0: dow = "Sunday"; break;
     case 1: dow = "Monday"; break;
     case 2: dow = "Tuesday"; break;
     case 3: dow = "Wednesday"; break;
     case 4: dow = "Thursday"; break;
     case 5: dow = "Friday"; break;
     case 6: dow = "Saturday"; break;
}

switch(month)
{
     case 0: month = "January"; break;
     case 1: month = "February"; break;
```

```
            case 2: month = "March"; break;
            case 3: month = "April"; break;
            case 4: month = "May"; break;
            case 5: month = "June"; break;
            case 6: month = "July"; break;
            case 7: month = "August"; break;
            case 8: month = "September"; break;
            case 9: month = "October"; break;
            case 10: month = "November"; break;
            case 11: month = "December"; break;
}


if(hour >=  12)
{
        hour = hour -12;
        amPm = "p.m.";
}


if(hour = = 0)
        hour = 12;


if(mins<10)
        mins = "0" + mins;


alert("Today is " + dow + ", " + month + " " + dom
+ ", " +
        year + ". The time is " + hour + ":" + mins
+ " " + amPm);
</script>
```

Arrays

As programs become more complex, more variables are needed. An easy way to keep these variables neatly organized is with arrays. Programmers can create their own arrays and place whatever they want into them. Once an array is populated, more elements can be added without problems—unlike other languages.

The first step is to create the array, name it, and define how large it should be. The array itself is just another variable, so it looks like setting up any other variable. After naming the array, use brackets to define an empty array:

```
var arrayName = [ ];
```

Now that you have created an array with nothing in it, each element can be defined:

```
arrayName[0] = "something";
arrayName[1] = "stuff";
```

Remember that an array of size 2 has elements 0 and 1. In JavaScript, it is okay to add more elements than the size of the array as the array will automatically become one element larger. Another way to do the same thing is to add all the elements when the array is created.

Instead of leaving the brackets empty, put the array's desired content in the brackets:

```
var arrayName= ["something", "stuff",…];
```

Since arrays are objects, they contain properties and methods. An important property of arrays is **.length**. As with string objects, length returns the number of items in an object. The first index in an array is 0, so the last one is always one less than total number of elements in the array. This can be written as:

```
arrayName.length-1;
```

Knowing the length of an array is useful when an element needs to be added to the end of an array and the exact size is unknown or has changed. Since the last element in an array is length-1, the next element added would be at length. This can be written as:

```
arrayName[arrayName.length] = someValue;
```

length is also used when using a loop to run through every element in an array. A *for loop* starting at 0 and ending at the array's length-1 is best suited for array. The following code will add *someValue* to every element in *arrayName*, regardless of the array's size.

```
for( var i = 0; i < arrayName.length; i++ )
{
        arrayName[ i ] = someValue;
}
```

Arrays also have methods, which are useful in many situations. They can save time by eliminating the need to write code to perform these tasks. Examples include the **.sort( )** and **.reverse( )** methods. *Sort* arranges the elements in alphabetical order, and *reverse* flips the order of the elements in the array. These methods can be used together to first alphabetize the array and then flip it so the elements store in reverse alphabetical order, like this:

```
var newArray = arrayName.sort( ).reverse( );
```

Other useful methods can be found in the *appendix*. They can do things like combine multiple arrays, add or subtract elements to the beginning or end of an array while shifting the position of the other elements, remove elements that have certain values, and so on.

Searches

An array can hold a large list of data, and it is useful to be able to search through the entire list to see if it contains certain values. Linear search and binary search are two popular search methods. A **linear search** starts are the beginning and checks each element of the list one by one until it finds the item it is searching for. This algorithm is simple to write and is extremely fast if the list is small or the item is near the beginning of the list. If the list is long and the item is either not in the list or near the end, it can be "expensive," meaning it takes up a lot of memory. An advantage of linear search is that the list does not need to be in order.

A **binary search** works more like a game of higher or lower. By guessing the middle value of a possible range, a player can reduce the possibilities by half. Doing this repeatedly rapidly narrows down the possibilities, so guessing 50 when trying to figure out a number between 1 and 100 will eliminate half the range. If the solution is lower than 50 then 50 – 100 can be taken out of consideration. Guessing 25 next will cut the range in half again. A binary search works in the same way, so in order for it to function, the list must already be sorted. Because it doesn't have to check each item one by one, binary searches are usually less expensive than linear searches, especially with large data sets. Sorting the arrays first can be expensive, however, so there are trade offs between these two methods of searching.

Functions

There will be times when certain blocks of code might be used in different places in a program. Instead of rewriting this code multiple times, a function can be created. A function is like a method, except the programmer sets up exactly what happens when a function runs. The best place to put these functions is in the head of the HTML file. To create a function, simply write the word *function* followed by the name you want to give the function. Make sure the name is not already being used by any JavaScript methods or keywords. The name is followed by parentheses, which can be used to accept parameters. The function is then opened—like loops and if statements—with a brace. Inside the function there can be as much or as little code as necessary. The function ends with a return statement and a closing brace. The return statement is followed by whatever needs to be sent back to the place where the function was called. For functions that do not need to return anything, simply write the word **return;** followed by a semicolon, or leave it out altogether. The function will automatically return with no value when it hits the closing brace.

```
function nameTheFunc( )
{
        //as much code as needed...
        return someValue;//optional if nothing is being returned
}
```

Now that the function has been created, it can be used whenever it's desired by using the line: **nameTheFunc( );** or whatever the programmer named it.

```
function myFunc( )
    {
            var firstName = "Bob";
            var lastName = "Smith";
            return firstName + lastName;
    }
```

Like methods, functions can also take one or more parameters. Simply name the parameters in the parentheses and separate them by commas if needed. A local copy of this variable can then be used anywhere inside of the function.

```
function anotherFunc( firstName, lastName )
{
        var fullName = firstName + " " +
                            lastName;
        return lastName;
}
```

Note: all the variables in this example are considered local and can only be used inside the function. If fullName is used outside this function then an error will occur—unless there is another local variable somewhere with the same name. This error can be avoided by using a global variable that all the code can see. To make a variable global, define it at the top of the JavaScript, above any functions.

```
var fullName;
function anotherFunc( firstName, lastName )
{
        fullName = firstName + " " + lastName;
        return lastName;
}
```

The only difference between these two examples is "var fullName" is defined as a variable before the function in the second example.

Therefore "var fullName" does not need to be defined within the function. Because the variable fullName is global in this example, any function in the document can use and modify it.

Events

Events are like messages or flags that objects can use to tell each other their state. The events discussed here are ones that tell when an action, such as clicking a button or moving the mouse over a picture, is performed by the user. Events are used as attributes of HTML tags, where they allow the programmer to run one line of JavaScript. There are many events, but the ones that will be most useful now are *onclick, onmouseover, onmouseout,* and *ondblclick.* The most common of these is the *onclick* event, which will run one line of code when added to a button (or picture—it works with any tag). This event is in the HTML code, not the JavaScript! In other words, the programmer must manually go into the code and find where the button is located. The easiest way to do this is by using the split view in the HTML editor. When the button is clicked, it should highlight the button's HTML code. Now, at the end of this opening tag (before the **>**) add the line **onclick = "yourFunction( )"**.

This event should still be inside the tag:

```
<input type = "button" …  onclick =
"yourFunction( )" >
```

If a button has been added previously then this tag already exists. There is no need to write it out again. The other three events work in much the same way. *ondblclick* will run the code if the button is double clicked. o*nmouseover* and *onmouseout* will run the code when the mouse hovers over the button and when the mouse leaves the button respectively. It is possible to have more than one event on a single button, such as *onmouseover* and *onmouseout*.

Document Object

The document object, which is named *document*, is automatically loaded when the HTML file is opened in a browser. A useful method in the document object is **getElementById(str);** This method uses the *id* attribute of any HTML tags in the document. For example, if there were an image with the id: *myPicture*, it could be accessed using the following code:

```
document.getElementById("myPicture");
```

Element Objects

Element objects refer to the HTML elements within the document. Some elements are *body*, *h1*, *p*, and *input*. They are also called tags. These elements are typically referred to by their unique ID, as was seen above in the method **getElementById( )**. One important property of events is **innerHTML**. This property refers to the text in between the opening and closing tags of an element. In the HTML code: **<h1 id="myH1"> My Heading </h1>** the innerHTML is "My

Heading." Depending on which side of the assignment operator this property is on, it can either read or write to the document.

```
document.getElementById("myH1").innerHTML =
          "I Just Changed My Heading";
```

In this example, the *h1* would change from "My Heading" to "I Just Changed My Heading."

To save the current text in the *h1* tag with the *id* of *myH1* in a variable, the *innerHTML* would be on the right side of the assignment operator, as demonstrated in the following example:

```
var textInH1 =
document.getElementById("myH1").innerHTML;
```

Note: If there is text already existing in the innerHTML—as in the first example—and a value is assigned to it then it will be replaced.

Forms

Another aspect of functions that makes them great tools is their ability to change hundreds of lines of code into just one. As we've seen above, when events are used, they can only trigger a single line of code. HTML employs forms when using items such as text boxes, text areas, check boxes, radio buttons, select (dropdown) boxes, buttons, and many other useful tools. JavaScript can be used to add some functionality to these things. With buttons, the most important thing is being able to tell the code that it has been pressed. This is one place where events come into play. Functions allow these events to trigger more complicated actions than a single line of code would be able to carry out.

Form Options

Besides buttons, other items—such as radio buttons, check boxes, select boxes, and text areas—can also go into forms. The programmer needs to make sure that these items are in the forms and that the forms are named with an ID. It would be simpler if there were only one form on any given page. To name a form, just add an *id* attribute to the tag remembering that this is case-sensitive. Most editors automatically give forms and form elements a default ID. Make sure to check the tag so that there are not two *id* attributes.

Without JavaScript, form elements do not have any functionality. Using JavaScript, these buttons, boxes, and text areas can be used to gather information from the webpage. Like forms, these items all need names, so the programmer can reference them later using their *id* attributes. Usually, these elements are automatically named upon insertion.

Once the forms and fields are all named with *id*s, functions can be created in JavaScript to add functionality. In most cases, something will happen if one of the *checkboxes* is checked. For example, if the user is purchasing something, the function might add to a total. For this type of function, an *if statement* could be used. First, tell the computer to look at the open document. Next, tell the computer what element is being evaluated by using **getElementById( )**. Now that the computer knows what it is looking at, ask the computer if this box is checked or not. If the box is checked, the computer will return true, and if the box is unchecked, the computer will return false. Such an *if statement* would look something like this:

```
if( document.getElementById("checkbox").checked)
    {
                //do this if the box is checked…
                //.checked returns true of false so no need to
                //write == true
    }
```

Radio buttons are like checkboxes except for one major difference: Radio buttons are all linked together. In other words, when one radio button is checked, no other button can be. To keep radio buttons connected, they are stored in an *array*. If five radio buttons are added, they will probably have names like R1[0], R1[1], R1[2], R1[3], and R1[4]. R1 is the name of the array. Each button is stored as an element in this array, starting at zero. To call on an element, square brackets are used [ ]. To show these radio button in an ID, they would be R1_0, R1_1, R1_2, R1_3, and R1_4. Even though there are five buttons, the highest element is four because they start at zero.

The *if statement* for a radio button looks like this:

```
if( document.getElementById("R1_0").checked )
{
        //do this if the box is checked…
}
```

Select (dropdown) boxes work like radio buttons in that the input they collect is saved in an array. The dropdown box itself is the array, and each option is an element. One attribute of select boxes is *selected*, which can be true or false. By using the method **.selectedIndex**, the index of the element that is currently selected will be returned (it will return *-1* if nothing is selected). The **.option** property can be used to call attributes of the individual options, but in most cases, simply using the **.value** property on the array is enough:

```
document.getElementById("select").value;
```

.value returns the selected element's value. Each element's value needs to be put in the array by adding an attribute or using the property pallet in an editor.

In cases where information needs to be retrieved or sent to a **text field,** simply assign a value to the text field or assign the text field to a new variable. Remember that whatever is on the lefthand side of the equals sign is being assigned a value. To save the content of the text field, type something along the lines of:

```
var stuff =
        document.getElementById("textfield").value;
```

To put something into the text area:

```
document.getElementById("textfield").value =
        "This will show up in the text area!";
```

With the skills introduced above, you'll be ready to start making websites that are more interactive than those made with HTML and CSS alone, but the principals of programming—including the development process, the use of variables, and iteration—will enable you to better grasp how computers "think" and to understand how software developers approach a problem.

In the preceding eight units, we've had the opportunity to become acquainted with the foundations of computing and to learn a set of practical skills that will enable you to used computers more creatively and more effectively. If you've made it this far, you have become a better informed and more skilled computer user, but you have also gained skills and knowledge that could make you a better artist, a more productive worker, and a more informed citizen. Computers have become central to modern society in a way that few imagined even a few decades ago. By mastering the principals of computer science, you are now better equipped to navigate the society we all share.

Important Vocabulary

- **AND** – basic logic gate where every part of a statement must be true for the entire statement to be true

- **Constant** – used in coding to store a value that cannot be changed

- **Debugging** – finding errors in code

- **Design – Implement – Test** – the three steps of the iterative development process

- **Incremental** – done in small chunks

- **Iterative** – continuously repeating steps, achieved in programming by using loops

- **OR** – basic logic gate where any part of a statement can be true for the entire statement to be true

- **Selection** – the logic structure in programming that uses *if statements* to select certain values

- **Sequence** – the structure that runs one line after another in order

- **Variable** – used in coding to store a value that can change

Appendix 1 – AP® Performance Task: Explore

Overview

Computing innovations impact our lives in ways that require considerable study and reflection for us to fully understand them. In this Performance Task, you will explore a computing innovation of your choice. A computing innovation is an innovation that includes a computer or program code as an integral part of its functionality. Your close examination of this computing innovation will deepen your understanding of computer science principles.

You will be provided with a minimum of 8 hours of class time to develop, complete, and submit the following:

- Computational Artifact
- Written Responses

General Requirements

This performance task requires you to select and investigate a computational innovation to:

- Analyze a computing innovations impact on society, economy, or culture and explain how this impact could be beneficial and/or harmful

- Explain how a computing innovation consumes, produces, or transforms data
- Describe how a data storage, data privacy, or data security concerns are raised based on the capabilities of the computing innovation

You are required to:

- Investigate your computing innovation using a variety of sources (e.g. print, online, expert interviews).
- Provide in-text citations of at least three sources that helped you create your computational artifact and/or formulate your written responses.
  - At least two of the sources must be available online or in print; your third source may be either online, in print, or a personal interview with an expert on the computing innovation.
  - At least two of the sources must have been created after the end of the previous academic year.
- Produce a computational artifact that illustrates, represents or explains the computing innovation's intended purpose, its function, or its effect.
- Provide written responses to questions about your computational artifact and computing innovation.

Submission Guidelines

1. Computational Artifact

Your computational artifact must provide an illustration, representation, or explanation of the computing innovation's intended purpose, its function, or its effect. The computational artifact must not simply repeat the information supplied in the written responses and should be primarily non-textual.

Submit a video, audio, or PDF file. Use computing tools and techniques to create one original computational artifact (a visualization, a graphic, a video, a program, or an audio recording). **Acceptable multimedia file types include .mp3, .mp4, .wmv, .avi, .mov, .wav, .aif, or .pdf format. PDFs must not exceed three pages. Video or audio files must not exceed 1 minute in length and must not exceed 30MB in size.**

2. Written Responses

Submit one PDF file in which you respond directly to each of the prompts below. **Clearly label your responses 2a–2e in order.** Your responses must provide evidence of the extensive knowledge you have developed about your chosen computing innovation and its impact(s). Write your responses so they would be understandable to someone who is not familiar with the computing innovation. Include citations, as applicable, within your written responses. **Your response to prompts 2a–2d combined must not exceed 700 words.** The references required in 2e are not included in the final word count.

2a. Provide information on your computing innovation and computational artifact.

- Name the computing innovation that is represented by your computational artifact.
- Describe the computing innovation's intended purpose and function.
- Describe how your computational artifact illustrates, represents, or explains the computing innovation's intended purpose, its function, or its effect.

(Must not exceed 100 words)

2b. Describe your development process, explicitly identifying the computing tools and techniques you used to create your artifact. Your description must be detailed enough so that a person unfamiliar with those tools and techniques will understand your process.

(Must not exceed 100 words)

Computing Innovation

2c. Explain at least one beneficial effect and at least one harmful effect the computing innovation has had, or has the potential to have, on society, economy, or culture.

(Must not exceed 250 words)

2d. Using specific details, describe:

- The data your innovation uses
- How the innovation consumes (as input), produces (as output), and/or transforms data
- At least one data storage concern, data privacy concern, or data security concern directly related to the computing innovation.

(Must not exceed 250 words)

References

2e. Provide a list of at least three online or print sources used to create your computational artifact and/or support your responses to the prompts provided in this performance task.

- At least two of the sources must have been created after the end of the previous academic year
- For each online source, include the complete and permanent URL. Identify the author, title, source, the date you retrieved the source, and, if possible, the date the reference was written or posted
- For each print source, include the author, title of excerpt/article and magazine or book, page number(s), publisher, and date of publication

- If you include an interview source, include the name of the person you interviewed, the date on which the interview occurred, and the person's position in the field
- Include in-text citations for the sources you used
- Each source must be relevant, credible, and easily accessed.

Scoring Guidelines

The Explore Performance Task will be evaluated based upon the 8 discrete criteria listed below. Each criterion is scored individually on a binary scale (i.e., each criterion can earn a score of 1 or 0) for a total of 8 possible points.

The first two criterion are evaluated based upon the computational artifact, using the written response as needed. The remaining six criteria are evaluated based upon the written response.

1 - Computational Artifact

- Identifies the computing innovation
                    AND

- Provides an illustration, representation, or explanation of the computing innovation's intended purpose, function, or effect

2 – Analyze the Impact of Computing (2a)

- States a fact about the correctly identified computing innovation's intended purpose OR function

3 – Analyze the Impact of Computing (2b)

- Identifies at least ONE effect of the identified or described computing innovation

4 – Analyze the Impact of Computing (2c)

- Identifies a beneficial effect of the identified or described computing innovation

AND

- Identifies a harmful effect of the identified or described computing innovation

5 – Analyze the Impact of Computing (2c)

- Explains how ONE of the identified effects relates to society, economy, or culture

6 – Analyzing Data and Information (2d)

- Identifies the data that the identified or described computing innovation uses
  AND

- Explains how that data is consumed, produced, OR transformed

7 – Analyzing Data and Information (2d)

- Identify one data storage, data privacy, OR data security concern related to the identified or described computing innovation

8 – Finding and Evaluation Information (2e/Artifact Written response)

- References, through in-text citation, at least 3 different sources

Appendix 2 – AP® Performance Task: Create

Overview

Programming is a collaborative and creative process that brings ideas to life through the development of software. Programs can help solve problems, enable innovations, or express personal interests. In this Performance Task, you will be developing a program of your choice. Your development process should include iteratively designing, implementing, and testing your program. You are strongly encouraged to work with another student in your class.

You will be provided with a minimum of 12 hours of class time to complete and submit the following:

- A video of your program running
- Individual written responses about your program and development process
- Program Code

General Requirements

This performance task requires you to develop a program on a topic that interests you or one that solves a problem. During the completion of this performance task, you will iteratively design, implement, and test your program. You will provide written responses to prompts about your program and specific program code that are significant to the functionality of your program. It is strongly recommended that a portion of the program involve some form of collaboration with another student in your class, for example, in the planning, designing, or testing (debugging) part of the development process. Your program development must also involve a significant amount of independent work writing code, in particular, algorithm(s) and abstraction(s) that you select to use as part of your written response to describe how the program code segments help your program run.

You are required to:

- Independently develop and algorithm that integrates two or more algorithms and that is fundamental for your program to achieve its intended purpose
- Develop an abstraction that manages the complexity of your program
- Create a video that displays the running of your program and demonstrates its functionality
- Write responses to all prompts in the performance task
- Submit your entire program code.

Program Requirements

Your program must demonstrate a variety of capabilities and implement several different language features that, when combined, produce a result that cannot easily be accomplished without computing tools and techniques. Your program should draw upon a combination of mathematical and logical concepts, such as use of numbers, variables, mathematical expressions with arithmetic operators, logical and Boolean operators and expressions, decision statements, iteration, and collections.

Your program must demonstrate:

- Use of several effectively integrated mathematical and logic concepts, from the language you are using
- Implementation of an algorithm that integrates two or more algorithms and integrates mathematical and/or logical concepts
- Development and use of abstraction to manage the complexity of your program (e.g., procedures, abstractions provided by the programming language, APIs)

Submission Guidelines

1. Video

Submit one video in .mp4, .wmv, .avi, or .mov format that demonstrates the running of at least one significant feature of your program. **Your video must not exceed 1 minute in length and must not exceed 30MB in size.**

2. Written Responses

Submit one PDF file in which you respond directly to each prompt. Clearly label your responses 2a–2d in order. **Your response to all** prompts combined must not exceed 750 words, exclusive of the Program Code.

Program Purpose and Development

2a. Provide a written response or audio narration in your video that:

- Identifies the programming language

- Identifies the purpose of your program

- Explains what the video illustrates

(Must not exceed 150 words)

2b. Describe the incremental and iterative development process of your program, focusing on two distinct points in that process. Describe the difficulties and/or opportunities you encountered and how they were resolved or incorporated. In your description clearly indicate whether the development described was collaborative or independent. At least one of these points must refer to independent program development.

(Must not exceed 200 words)

2c. Capture and paste the program code segment that implements an algorithm (marked with an oval in section 3 below) and that is fundamental for your program to achieve its intended purpose. This code segment must include an algorithm you developed individually on your own, must include two or more algorithms, and must integrate mathematical and/or logical concepts. Describe how each algorithm within your selected algorithm functions independently, as well as in combination with others, to form a new algorithm that helps to achieve the intended purpose of the program.

(Must not exceed 200 words)

2d. Capture and paste the program code segment that contains an abstraction you developed individually on your own (marked with a rectangle in section 3 below). This abstraction must integrate mathematical and logical concepts. Explain how your abstraction helped manage the complexity of your program.

(Must not exceed 200 words)

3. Program Code

Capture and paste your entire program code in this section.

- Mark with an **oval** the segment of program code that implements the algorithm you created for your program that integrates other algorithms and integrates mathematical and/or logical concepts

- Mark with a **rectangle** the segment of program code that represents an abstraction you developed

- Include comments or acknowledgment for program code that has been written by someone else

Scoring Guidelines

The Create Performance Task will be evaluated based upon the 8 discrete criteria listed below. Each criterion is scored individually on a binary scale (i.e., each criterion can earn a score of 1 or 0) for a total of 8 possible points.

1 – Developing a Program with a Purpose (Video Response, 2a)

- The video demonstrates the running of at least one feature of the program submitted

AND

- The response (audio narration or written response) identifies the purpose of the program (what the program is attempting to do)

2 – Developing a Program with a Purpose (2b)

- Describes or outlines steps used in the incremental and iterative development process to create the entire program

3 – Developing a Program with a Purpose (2b)

- Specifically identifies at least two program development difficulties or opportunities.

AND

- Describes how the two identified difficulties or opportunities are resolved or incorporated

4 – Applying Algorithms (Code Segment in 2c)

- Selected code segment implements an algorithm

5 – Applying Algorithms (2c)

- Selected code segment implements an algorithm that uses mathematical or logical concepts
  AND

- Explains how the selected algorithm functions
  AND

- Describes what the selected algorithm does in relation to the overall purpose of the program.

6 – Applying Algorithms (2c)

- Selected code segment implements an algorithm that includes at least two or more algorithms
  AND

- At least one of the included algorithms uses mathematical or logical concepts
  AND

- Explains how one of the included algorithms functions independently.

7 – Applying Abstraction (Code Segment in 2d)

- Selected code segment is a student-developed abstraction.

8 – Applying Abstraction (2d)

- Explains how the selected abstraction manages the complexity of the program.

Appendix 3 – JavaScript Objects

String Object

var *yourVar* = "a string";

yourVar.METHOD( );

String Object Properties

Property	Description
length	Returns the number of **characters** in the string

String Object Methods

Method	Description
toUpperCase( )	Returns the string in all uppercase letters
toLowerCase( )	Returns the string in all lowercase letters
charAt(int)	Returns what character is at the specified index

substring(int1, int2)	Returns the string from index **int1** to index **int2 -1**
substring(int)	Returns the string from index **int** to the last character of the string
concat(str1, str2, ...)	Combines two or more stings together
sup( )	Changes the string into a superscript
sub( )	Changes the string into a subscript
parseInt(str)	Changes the string into an integer
parseFloat(str)	Changes the string into a floating-point number (decimal)

Math Object

Math.METHOD( );

Math Object Properties

Property	Description
E	Returns Euler's constant (approx. 2.718)
LN2	Returns the natural logarithm of 2 (approx. 0.693)
LN10	Returns the natural logarithm of 10 (approx. 2.302)
LOG2E	Returns the base-2 logarithm of E (approx. 1.414)
LOG10E	Returns the base-10 logarithm of E (approx. 0.434)
PI	Returns PI (approx. 3.14159)
SQRT1_2	Returns the square root of 1/2 (approx. 0.707)
SQRT2	Returns the square root of 2 (approx. 1.414)

Math Object Methods

Method	Description
abs(num)	Returns the absolute value of a number
ceil(num)	Returns the value of a number rounded upwards to the nearest integer
floor(num)	Returns the value of a number rounded downwards to the nearest integer
round(num)	Rounds a number to the nearest integer
min(num1, num2, ...)	Returns the number with the lowest value of x and y
max(num1, num2, ...)	Returns the number with the highest value of x and y
sqrt(num)	Returns the square root of a number
pow(num, num)	Returns the value of x to the power of y

random( )	Returns a random number between 0 and 1 (excluding 1)
sin(num)	Returns the sine of a number
cos(num)	Returns the cosine of a number
tan(num)	Returns the tangent of an angle

Document & HTML Objects

document.METHOD( );

Document Object Properties

Property	Description
bgColor	Sets or returns the color of the background
fgColor	Sets or returns the color of the foreground
title	Returns the title of the current document

cookie	Sets or returns all cookies associated with the current document
domain	Returns the domain name for the current document
lastModified	Returns the date and time a document was last modified
referrer	Returns the URL of the document that loaded the current document
URL	Returns the URL of the current document

Document Object Methods

Method	Description
getElementById("*id*")	Returns the element of a specific HTML tag using specified ID

blur( )	Takes focus off the element
focus( )	Gives focus to the element
click( )	Simulates a mouse click on the element

Element Object Properties

innerHTML	Sets text in between the opening and closing of specific HTML tags
style	Sets or returns the value of the style attribute of an element
className	Sets or returns the value of the class attribute of an element

Date Object

var *yourObj* = new **Date**( );

var *newVar* = *yourObj.METHOD*( );

Date Methods

Method	Description
Date( )	Returns today's date and time
getDate( )	Returns the day of the month from a Date object (from 1-31)
getDay( )	Returns the day of the week from a Date object (from 0-6)
getMonth( )	Returns the month from a Date object (from 0-11)
getFullYear( )	Returns the year, as a four-digit number, from a Date object
getHours( )	Returns the hour of a Date object (from 0-23)
getMinutes( )	Returns the minutes of a Date object (from 0-59)
getSeconds( )	Returns the seconds of a Date object (from 0-59)

getMilliseconds( )	Returns the milliseconds of a Date object (from 0-999)
getTime( )	Returns the number of milliseconds since midnight Jan 1, 1970. Also, known as Internet Time.

Array Object

var *yourArray* = [ ];

yourArray[0] = *something*;

yourArray[1] = *somethingElse*;

...

yourArray.METHOD( );

Array Object Properties

Property	Description
length	Returns the number of elements in the array

Array Object Methods

Method	Description
concat(A_1, A_2,...)	Combines two or more arrays and returns an array

reverse( )	Reverses the order of the array and returns an array
join(str)	Changes the array into a string and separates them with the specified string and returns a string
sort( )	Rearranges the array in alphabetical or numerical order and returns an array
push( )	Adds new elements to the end of an array, and returns the new length
pop( )	Removes the last element of an array, and returns that element
shift( )	Removes the first element of an array, and returns that element
unshift( )	Adds new elements to the beginning of an array, and returns the new length
splice(num and/or str)	Adds/Removes elements from an array

slice(int1 , int2)	Selects a part of an array, and returns the new array from index int1 to index int2-1

Events

Place the event followed by an equal sign and a function inside of an HTML tag.

<SOMETAG ... anEvent = "yourFunction( )">

Event	Description
onclick	When the mouse is clicked
ondblclick	When the mouse is double clicked
onkeypress	When a key on the keyboard is pressed
onkeydown	When a key on the keyboard is pressed down
onkeyup	When a key on the keyboard is released
onload	When the page is loaded
onreset	When the refresh button is pressed

onresize	When the page is resized
onselect	When text on the page is selected
onsubmit	When the submit button is pressed
onunload	When the page is closed
onmouseover	When the mouse is over the element
onmouseout	When the mouse is taken off an element
onmouseup	When the mouse button is released
onmousedown	When the mouse button is pressed down
onmousemove	When the mouse moves
onerror	When an error occurs on the page

Important Vocabulary for the AP® Computer Science Principles Exam

AND – basic logic gate where every part of a statement must be true for the entire statement to be true

Applications – includes word processors, photo editing software, web browsers, games, music programs, and almost everything else on the computer excluding saved files

ARPANET – the Advanced Research Projects Agency Network, first agency to use TCP/IP

ASCII – American Standard Code for Information Interchange

Asymmetric Key Encryption – a different key is used to encrypt and decrypt a message

Bandwidth – the amount of resources available to transmit the data

Big Data – sets of data that are larger than a consumer software application can handle

Binary – base 2, number system that uses 0, 1

BIOS – Basic input/output system

Bit – each number in the binary system, 0 or 1

Bit Rate – the number of bits that can be processed per second

Byte – 8 bits

Caesar Cipher – a shift cipher where each letter is shifted the same amount

Central Processing Unit (CPU) – carries out every command or process on the computer and can be thought of as the brain of the computer

Cipher – is a pair of algorithms that give details on how to encrypt and decrypt the data

Client – any computer that requests a service

Cloud Computing – using a remote server to store files

CMYK – color model used for printing. Stands for **c**yan, **m**agenta, **y**ellow, and black (**key**), where the number associated with each letter is the percentage of each color used

Computationally hard – a problem that takes too long even for a computer to find the exact solution

Computer – an electronic device that processes data according to a set of instructions or commands, known as a program

Constant – used in coding to store a value that cannot be changed

Core – the central processing unit (CPU) and the main memory

CSS – Cascading Style Sheets, redefines mark-up in HTML

DDoS – distributed denial-of-service attack, hackers flood a site with fake request making all the site's recourses unavailable for legitimate users

Debugging – finding errors in code

Decimal – base 10, number system that used 0-9

Decryption – the reverse process of encryption

Design – Implement – Test – the three steps of the iterative development process

Digit – each number in the decimal system, 0-9

Digital Certificate – a trusted third-party file that verifies a site as legitimate

Digital signature – an electronic signature that, by using public key, can be verified authentic

DNS – Domain Name System, one of the smaller networks that make up the Internet. It contains many servers that act like phone books

Domain Name – a name given or linked to an IP address

Encryption – taking text and converting it so it is illegible

Fault Tolerant – a property of IP. If there is an error, it still works properly

FTP – File Transfer Protocol, used for transferring files between a client and a server

Hacker – anyone who uses their technological skills to solve problems. A malicious security hacker exploits weaknesses on a computer or network and can steal or disrupt data

Hardware – the physical parts of the computer, including devices such as the monitor, keyboard, speakers, wires, chips, cables, plugs, disks, printers, and mice

Heuristic approach – an approach that gives results that are "good enough" when an exact answer is not necessary.

Hexadecimal – base 16, number system that uses 0-9 and a-f

HTML – Hyper Text Markup Language, the standard for creating web pages

HTTP – Hyper Text Transfer Protocol, used for websites

HTTPS – a secure version of HTTP that uses SSL/TLS

IMAP – Internet Message Access Protocol, used for e-mail

Incremental – done in small chunks

Input and output (I/O) devices – how the user interacts with the computer

Internet – a network of smaller networks connected using a specific set of rules that computers use to communicate with each other

IP – Internet protocol, a unique address for every device connected to the Internet

IP Address – a unique identifier for every device on the Internet

IPv4 – the version of IP that uses 32-bit addresses

IPv6 – the version of IP that uses 128-bit addresses

ISP – Internet Service Provider

Iterative – continuously repeating steps, achieved in programming by using loops

Key – in cryptography, a shared secret to make encryption harder to crack

Latency – the amount of delay when sending digital data over the Internet or the round-trip time information takes to get from the client to the server and back

Lossless – data compression that does not lose data during compression

Lossy – data compression that loses data during compression

MAC (media access control) Address – a unique, physical address that is stored in the computer's ROM

Main memory – memory that temporarily stores information while it is being sent to the CPU, also called RAM

Metadata – additional data about the main data, usually at the beginning of a file

Modem - a device that handles both the modulation and the demodulation of signals

Modular arithmetic – using the remainder when dividing, also known as clock arithmetic

Motherboard (logic board) - the standardized printed circuit board that connects the CPU, main memory, and peripherals

Name Server – a server that contains many IP addresses and their matching domain names

Network – a group of computers that are connected so they can share resources using a data link

Nonvolatile – does not need a power supply. Information is physically written to the device

Nybble (or Nibble) – half of a byte, 4 bits

One-way Function - a problem that is easy in one direction and difficult in the other

Operating System – the visual representation of the computer

OR – basic logic gate where any part of a statement can be true for the entire statement to be true

Packets – small chunks of data used in TCP/IP

Peripherals – the input and output (I/O) devices and the secondary memory

Phishing – using "bait" to trick the user into entering sensitive information like user names, passwords, or credit card numbers

Pixelation – when individual pixels are too large and the image begins to look blocky

POP – Post Office Protocol, used for e-mail

POST – Power-on self-test

Power Supply – converts AC electricity to the lower voltage DC electricity that is needed to power the computer

Private Key – a shared secret needed to decrypt a message

Protocol – a specific set of rules

Public Key – a system that allows a key to be publicly published

Random Access Memory (RAM) – memory that can be retrieved or written to anywhere without having to go through all the previous memory

RGB – color model used for most monitors or screens. Stands for red, green, and blue, referring to the color of light

Root Name Server – one of thirteen servers that contain every IP address and its matching domain name

Router – a networking device that routes Internet traffic to the destination

Sample Rate – how often an analog signal is used when converting to digital, usually measured in bits per second

Secondary Memory – used for long term storage and is physically changed when files are saved or deleted

Selection – the logic structure in programming that uses *if* statements to select certain values

Sequence – the structure that runs one line after another in order

Sequential Memory – memory used to store back-up data on a tape

Server – any computer that provides a service

Software – includes the operating system and the applications. It is usually stored on a computer's hard drive and cannot physically be touched. At the lowest level, it is a series of ones and zeros

SSL – Secure Sockets Layer, issues digital certificates for websites

Subdomain – precedes the domain name, owned by the domain *https://subdomain.domain.com*

Substitution Cipher – a cipher where a letter is mapped or swapped with another letter in the alphabet

Symmetric Key Encryption – the same key is used to encrypt and decrypt a message

TCP – Transmission Control Protocol, a set of rules for breaking down requests into smaller, more manageable, numbered packets

TLS – Transport Layer Security, issues digital certificates for websites

UDP – User Datagram Protocol, like TCP and usually used for streaming audio/video

URL – Uniform Resource Locator, specifies where to find a file on a domain

Variable – used in coding to store a value that can change

Virus – a program that infects other programs and usually spreads to other programs or computers by copying itself repeatedly

VoIP – Voice over Internet Protocol, used for telephony

Volatile – needs a power supply. Turning off the power deletes information

Web (World Wide Web) – the part of the Internet that uses HTTP and HTTPS

Made in the USA
San Bernardino, CA
23 May 2019